# Answers May Vary

## Essays on Teaching English as a Second Language

---

## Dorothy E. Zemach

---

WAYZGOOSE PRESS

ISBN-10: 1938757068
ISBN-13: 978-1-938757-06-8

Edited by Dorothy E. Zemach.
Cover design by DJ Rogers.
Published in the United States by Wayzgoose Press.

*Note: These essays were originally published in the "From A to Z" column in Essential Teacher, the magazine of TESOL, the international organization for the teaching of English as a second or foreign language. Visit TESOL's website to learn more about this organization. A full listing of the articles and the dates they originally appeared can be found at the end of this book.*

# Table of Contents

# uve got mail!!

My mother-in-law still refers to the emails we send her as faxes, and, in fact, when her daughter can coax her into typing a message on the computer, she sends short, fact-filled messages that seem indeed more like faxes than like letters. But the emails I get from my students – matriculated into regular university classes – are more like vanity license plates. Rife with spelling, punctuation, and grammar errors, the friendliness nonetheless shines through: "Hi dorthy!!! How r u? Im so sorry my absent!!! please forgive me ok!!" My favorite one, which I have saved, opens with "oh my goddess!!!" (He may have meant, *Oh, my goodness!*, but because I'll never know for sure, I'm free to give it any interpretation I like.) These students, I should say, carefully proofread their papers and even their informal in-class writing assignments.

What causes these high-level, hardworking students to write in symbols? Why do they remove punctuation from the middle of a sentence and heap it up at the end? Perhaps they are carrying over techniques from text messaging on cell phones, on which every character takes up space and costs money. They may be unable to perceive the levels of formality between student and professor in a university where even tenured professors wear jeans and go by their first names. They may simply be writing quickly (email is supposed to be fast, isn't it?), or perhaps they are imitating the messages they receive from their friends, both international and U.S.

Nonstandard spelling is by no means limited to international students: In an undergraduate grammar class I once taught in a university English department, some students who respectfully called me "Professor Zemach" in class, then sent follow-up emails that started with "Hi!!!" and closed with "Luv ya!!" My 9-year-old niece emails me messages I almost have to read out loud to decipher, asking if I feel "gr8."

If this informal style of email writing is common even among native speakers, then why not let international students carry on? To me, it's a question of register. Whether they wear blue jeans or not, professors are still professors, and a student who acts respectfully will normally be thought better of than one who doesn't. Emails that do not use capital letters and standard punctuation and that contain many grammatical errors are simply harder to read – easier to write, no doubt, but harder to read. Learners of English need to learn where the burden of communication mostly lies – with the speaker and the writer, and with the lower status communicator. And although I would accept almost any message at all from my niece, I felt uncomfortable with "Hiya, Zebra" (from a U.S. student, who most certainly had my surname spelled correctly on his syllabus) and "i know i dint show up this morning im gonna have 2 midterms for other classes this week and im a little tired" (from an international student with a TOEFL score of over 500).

The writing curriculum here at the University of Oregon is probably not much different from that in other colleges and universities; we focus mainly on the content, organization, and style of academic papers. We have no unit or chapter in a textbook or course pack that specifically instructs students how to send email to their professors. Indeed, I don't know of many academic writing books that address this issue (one high-level exception is *Academic Writing for Graduate Students* [Swales & Feak, 1994]). So I sent every student in my class a message on university email etiquette, from openings ("It's OK for me to open with *Hi Jasmine –* ; the student should respond with *Dear Dorothy*") to final editing ("You should always spellcheck an email that is being sent to someone who is eventually going to assign you a grade for your English ability."). I pointed out what I do to make sure my messages to students are polite: I check the spelling of their names carefully; I use short, clear sentences; I communicate essential information first.

My students responded positively. "I didn't know this before. Thanx!" wrote one student gratefully (or ironically? I can always hope!), and several confessed that they had never sent an email to their non-ESL professors because they were unsure of how to write one. In some classes, the message led to an in-class discussion of levels of politeness in U.S. universities and the differences in language used among students and between students and professors. We discussed the impressions students might make if they used very formal language when sending emails to their friends, and I gave examples of different styles I use in work-related emails.

I don't think we need to worry about international students learning to write emails that are more appropriate than those sent by U.S. students any more than we need to worry that our students sometimes have a better handle on writing clear topic sentences and thesis statements. I want my students to be able to communicate effectively with a variety of English speakers: other students, professors, potential employers.

Until writing textbooks include this kind of information, the instruction is left to us. As you send and receive email, pay attention to the style of the letters. With whom are you most formal? When might you leave off a salutation or a closing? What effect do letters with poor grammar or nonstandard language have on you? (I have an editor who closes her letters with "Hugs, L"; but it's probably significant that she is paying me, not the other way around).

Share your impressions with your students. I'm sure they'll be gr8ful.

**Reference**

Swales, J. M., & Feak, C. (1994). *Academic writing for graduate students*. Ann Arbor: The University of Michigan Press.

# Read to the End

I used to teach a university academic reading class made up of matriculated students with various majors. The variety of students made it difficult to choose reading materials that would be interesting to all of them (let alone me). For reading skills and vocabulary, all the students used the same textbook, but for fluency practice each student selected his or her own book, read it outside of class, and wrote a report at term's end. My only requirements for the book were that it be over 200 pages long, not assigned for another class, and interesting.

First, students had to select a book. I had naively thought that this stage would be the easiest; students who didn't know titles in English would just tell me what they liked to read in their own language, and I would recommend a similar book in English. I was unprepared for how many of my students (willing enrollees in a university, mind you) claimed they liked to read nothing at all in any language. Some could be persuaded to pick books based on movies or television shows they liked; one chose a book based on – yes – his favorite video game. One student, who'd always struck me as rather, well, lightweight, had selected Tolkien's *The Fellowship of the Ring* (1954/1999). I was pretty impressed until I overheard her say that she'd chosen it because it was the only English book in her apartment (left by her ex-boyfriend), and she didn't want to talk to him in order to return it.

Another young woman brought in a tedious,

preachy volume on marketing strategies from her business class, written mainly in sports metaphors and popular slang. I reminded her that she couldn't use books from other classes and again stressed that she should choose something interesting to her personally. She came back the following lesson with *Good in Bed* (Weiner, 2002).

I planned a few intermediate checkpoints during the term, days when students would be responsible for sharing some of what they'd read so far in small groups. That would at least prompt people to begin so they would have something to say. Those students who hadn't read far were usually impressed (or shamed?) by how much other classmates had read, and this gave them renewed motivation.

One discussion item was a prediction of what would happen later in their books. As I was passing one group, I heard a student (I'll call him *Jay*) say, in a rather bored and smug tone, "Oh, it will end happily. These kinds of books always do." He had a point, but because I wanted the students to see the positive aspects of predictability as well, I stopped and guided the group through a discussion of what typical plot elements they might find in U.S. and English novels, why authors would make use of familiar plot lines, when and why they might break away from these molds, and so on. I finished by asking Jay to note, as he read, how he felt as he noticed his predictions coming true. As I left the group, I finally thought to ask him what book he was reading. "*Lord of the Flies*," he replied (Golding, 1959).

What did they learn? Even more than I'd expected. Every student reported an increase in reading speed, and all the students commented on how their ability to guess words from context and decide which words were worth looking up had improved.

One of the many readers of J. K. Rowling's *Harry Potter* series, a graduate student, noted,

*I didn't catch and grasp many words related to people's basic and physical movement and speech. All of the words I have memorized and studied through English textbook or practice books for English exam cannot follow the words like this: clamber, grunt, mumble, blurt, bang, swap, scream, gasp, stray, wail, snooze, mutter, sneer, lurch* [and three more lines of similar words]. *Do all kids understand those words? If they have my vocabulary quiz, what score will they get?*

He was right, of course – none of those words came up in our vocabulary textbook or could be figured out from Latin or Greek roots and affixes; yet they are common, useful words.

The *Good in Bed* reader wrote,

*To be honest, I felt pretty comfortable reading this book. Of course, I am sure to have missed many senses, many jokes in which slang was used; but except that, I am sure to have understood the main part of it. I didn't want to waste my time checking every single word in the dictionary; so, I just used it when I really needed it to understand the sense of a sentence or if I felt I could use this word while speaking. When a grammat-*

*ical structure seemed new to me, I wrote it down and tried to remember it. … Since I started reading this book, my friends tend to say that I am speaking as an essay! But whatever they say, I am glad my English is better off … .*

Could any reading teacher hope for more?

And what of Jay? In his words,

*In conclusion,* Lord of the Flies *is not the same as* Lord of the Rings. *At first I was very happy to find this famous book so thin. But I learned that it is important to read the end of things even books titles. Now I will try to finish my other class's assignments too.*

## References

Golding, W. (1959). *Lord of the flies.* New York: Perigee.

Tolkien, J.R.R. (1999). *The fellowship of the ring.* New York: Houghton Mifflin. (Original work published 1954)

Weiner, J. (2002). *Good in bed.* New York: Simon & Schuster.

# That's My English

When students ask how I can tell if a paper is plagiarized, I tell them I can smell it – and Hyun Jae's paper reeked (names have been changed to protect the guilty). He'd clearly taken most of his book report on *Harry Potter* (Rowling, 1998) off various Internet sites; one dead giveaway was that he hadn't changed the capital letters at the beginnings of sentences when he pasted them onto other sentences, as in "In the book, *Harry Potter and The Sorcerer's Stone*, Written by J. K. Rollings, I believe that courage is the most outstanding theme." And clearly he hadn't copied the author's name off the book itself. (Why is that while teachers mind plagiarism, they mind bad plagiarism even more?)

In my writing classes, I discuss plagiarism at great length, but this book report had been written for a reading class, where I had not discussed plagiarism. Hyun Jae may not have been aware that he'd done anything wrong, but it was unlikely: The assignment had asked for a brief, one- to two-paragraph plot summary and two pages on the student's personal reaction and application of various reading strategies. However, I still couldn't assign a grade to three pages of downloaded material, most of it not even very good, and none of which matched the assignment.

I knew from experience that no one likes to be accused of something that the teacher, at least, considers cheating and that sensitively explaining the problem and asking Hyun Jae to remedy it might take some time. So I emailed Hyun Jae and asked him to schedule a 20-minute appointment with me.

When he came to my office, even before sitting down he said, "I knew I shouldn't have copied my book report from the Internet." That took about 3 seconds. It took another 3–4 minutes to determine through a question-and-answer session that he had actually read the book and applied the reading strategies. I was done, but he made no move to leave. Fifteen minutes of our scheduled time remained, and he kept sitting there and looking at me expectantly. On an impulse, I asked, "Do you want to know how I caught you?" Curiosity proved stronger than embarrassment, and I had him come over to my computer with his paper.

I pointed out which sentences had struck me as not reflecting his voice and showed how I could type any string of seven words (put in between quotation marks) into a search engine like Google and come up with the Web site he'd copied from. He was fascinated and had me do this several times. Then he said, "Try one of my sentences." We found a string of seven words he'd written (with no grammatical errors), plugged them into Google, and – nothing. He looked most impressed and rather proud. "Wow. That's my English." We tried a few more times with his own phrases and never found a match.

If you've never done this, try it: Type "Written by J.K. Rollings, I believe that" into a Web search engine and see what you get. Isn't it amazing how many essay sites copy from each other? Then try a string of seven words from this article. A few strings of common words, such as "When he came to my office," will find matches, but they won't lead to an identical sentence, and most combinations will not bring any matches.

The search results led us to a discussion of how remarkable it is that, when so many people speak a language, you can still put seven words together and come up with something completely correct yet completely your own. English has not been used up; not everything worth saying has been said. We drew analogies to music (one can still write love songs) and art (one can still paint landscapes and portraits) and discussed the value of quoting others and being original. No doubt it was the most effective lesson on plagiarism I've ever given, even though it didn't happen in a classroom or as part of a planned lesson.

I offer the story of Hyun Jae to you as a lesson plan. Have the students discuss what his motivations might have been (his answer: he didn't start until the night before the assignment was due, and his U.S. roommate suggested this technique as a great timesaver; however, other equally plausible answers would be worth discussing in class), whether it was wrong, how he was caught, what he learned. I'm sure Hyun Jae would be flattered if his story could bring even one student to understand how he felt when he said, "That's my English."

## Reference

Rowling, J. K. (1998). *Harry Potter and the sorcerer's stone.* New York: Scholastic.

# Telling Tales

The other day I went with a Japanese graduate student (I'll call her Ayaka) to buy a cup of coffee from a snack bar on campus. "Do you want room?" asked the student behind the counter. (This means, in Eugene, Oregon, coffee-speech, room for cream, a little space left in the cup to add cream, milk, sugar, etc.).

"Yes, thank you," said Ayaka. She stepped aside, and I ordered my coffee.

"Do you want room?"

"No, that's OK," I answered.

I noticed Ayaka taking her cup right past the condiment table. "The cream is over there," I pointed out helpfully.

"Oh, I don't want any cream," she said. "I like my coffee black."

"But ... you told the girl that you *did* want cream," I said.

"Well, she offered me something, and I felt it would sound rude to say no. She won't know if I put in any cream or not, so it doesn't matter." I digested this remark as I walked over to the table to get some cream for my own coffee. This time Ayaka was surprised.

"But you said you didn't want cream."

"No," I corrected her, "I said I didn't want *room* for cream. That way I get more coffee. I take a little sip first, and then add the cream."

At this point I stop telling the story and ask the students to guess what Ayaka and I were thinking about each other. Sometimes I have them guess in groups, or sometimes we have a whole-class discussion, but inevitably the class comes up with (in different words) the following guesses:

Dorothy, thinking about Ayaka: "What a doormat. She's paying for the coffee, so why can't she say what she wants? If she can't tell someone how she wants her coffee, how will she negotiate choices with her studies, career, and family?"

Ayaka, thinking about Dorothy: "How cheap can you get? If she wants more coffee, why doesn't she buy a larger size? Will such a selfish person be able to have friends?"

The next step is to tease out the underlying cultural assumptions. This takes more time, of course, but by the end of an intensive discussion the class can arrive at some simple yet profound generalization, such as "In Japan, everyone looks out for others, and so everyone is taken care of. In the United States, everyone looks out for himself or herself, so everyone is taken care of."

Although we also discuss the dangers of generalizations, coming up with some helps students see that similar desires and motivations can manifest themselves in almost opposite ways.

But what's important for me as a teacher is not just the conclusion, which after all I could write on the board or find in a textbook. The important part is the story itself, the path to the conclusion. Stories are fascinating, and students will puzzle out the motivations of characters with far more interest than they will read a two-sentence summary at the end of a chapter.

Discussion with classmates sharpens critical-thinking skills while showing how many interpretations different people can have of the same events. Stories in books are good, but far more popular are stories that I tell, especially if they involve me (and especially if I don't come out looking too good!).

Another benefit of storytelling surfaced for me last fall, when I noticed that some of the students were disappearing after the mid-class break. Attendance wasn't required as long as they learned the material in some way, so perhaps I shouldn't have cared. But there's something damaging to the ego about students who've dipped in the water but don't want to swim. So I took to telling stories. I told half of a story just before the break and the conclusion just after. I broke off at an interesting or confusing part of the story and asked the students to guess what would happen or what would have explained someone's behavior. Then after the break, they shared their guesses, and I finished the story. Worked like a charm – everyone came back after the break, ready to talk.

Telling stories draws students in. They pay attention, think deeply, draw conclusions. And good stories are "telling": They reveal insights and truths. Stories are just as appropriate for skills classes as they are for content classes. Embed your stories with the target vocabulary and grammar, and students will happily drill themselves as they listen, ask questions, and discuss.

Not everyone has a collection of great stories, of course, or stories relevant to the class. My solution is simple: Make them up. Even true stories may need a little, ahem, adjustment to bring out the salient points. For example, in the opening story, just about the only truth left is that I like coffee. I never had a graduate student named Ayaka, I don't drink coffee with my students, and I prefer my coffee black. If you can't bring yourself to, well, lie, you can always say, "I read somewhere about a man who ..." or "I heard of someone who once ...." I keep a file in my desk of good stories that I can re-tell or adapt: clippings from newspapers and magazines, excerpts photocopied from books, and anecdotes circulated through email.

If you have not used stories before, I encourage you to try. Begin your class with "A funny thing happened on the way to class today" or "My cousin once had a strange experience while traveling."

May you enjoy telling tales, and may all your tales be telling ones.

# Grader's Block

I remember once trying to get through reading and grading a large stack of student essays. Every time I would pick one up and get to work, I'd be overcome with sleepiness – overwhelming sleepiness, the sort that makes your neck snap as your head plunges towards the desk. I'd get a cup of coffee, walk around the room, and lean out the window for some fresh air, but it made no difference. As soon as I started back in on that paper stack, it was as if I'd been hit from behind.

I emailed a nonteaching friend about this phenomenon, and she helpfully wrote back her assessment of the situation: "It's your subconscious telling you that you don't want to grade those papers." *Sub*conscious? Hey, I'm not that subtle. I knew I didn't want to grade those papers back when I assigned them. In fact, I knew it before I assigned them. I'd known it for years. And if I'd felt like it, I could have examined the various reasons I didn't want to grade them: the hours it would take, the boredom of reading many papers on the same topic, the frustration of knowing some students wouldn't respond to the comments, and the complaints I'd get from students who earned a B+ or lower.

But when you have that stack in front of you, your sleepiness and all the reasons for it are, so to speak, academic. You may have delayed with peer reviewing sessions and deadline extensions, but in the end, they've still got to be graded. I won't pretend I've found a foolproof solution. However, over the years – and over the stacks – I have found a few measures that help.

**Before the papers stack up:**

*Be realistic.* I know teachers who'd bend over backwards to accommodate their students' schedules and busy lives but still expect to collect 30 papers on Monday and hand them back on Wednesday. They feel exhausted if they do and guilty if they don't. Of course, it's not fair to keep papers all term, but remind yourself that students also deserve a careful reading for their papers, and you can't do that if you feel overwhelmed or run down. I've read before that students don't read the comments teachers write on their papers, but apparently the students I teach never read that research, and I've found that most of students read the comments, care about them, and often want to discuss them. So comments need to be written with a clear mind.

*Set your schedules carefully.* Do you really want to grade papers all weekend, or would it be better to grade during the week and take a real rest? Or perhaps you can only grade on weekends, when you have some quiet hours to yourself. Look at a calendar when you assign papers, and block out grading time.

*Make use of nonteaching times to collect and return papers.* Have students turn in papers when it's most convenient for you, even if you don't hold class that day. They can slip papers under a door, leave them in a box, or, if you're very fortunate, turn them in to a departmental secretary who can stamp them with the date. You can return papers out of class as well, by leaving them in an out box by your office door. I've even known teachers who accepted, marked, and returned papers entirely electronically.

**After the papers stack up**:

*Move to a different physical location.* This is my best tip: Simply sitting in a different place can perk you up remarkably. I routinely rotate among three or four favorite locations.

*Just move.* Going to the gym for an hour is just an avoidance technique, but walking around the building or up and down the hall can get your blood circulating enough to restore life to your brain cells.

*Have a snack.* I'm not suggesting cola and doughnuts, of course. But some fruit and nuts will provide quick energy. You already know if you're someone who skips meals (or nutritious meals) when busy or pressured. Just don't forget what to do about it.

*Save the best for last.* Keep a few papers from your top students as a reward for having dealt with the difficult ones first.

*Grade with a partner.* Grab another teacher who's got a

stack, and sit down together. Like exercising with a partner, grading together can motivate you both, and you can read amusing or interesting bits of papers aloud or ask each other for advice.

*Remove distractions.* If I grade near my computer, I know I'll be constantly interrupted with email, all of which (even the spam) somehow seems more important than the grading. When all else fails, I take only my stack and grade book to a coffee shop. Then I tell someone to meet me there two hours later. That way, I know I have to stay for two hours, and I have nothing else to do but grade (and the coffee doesn't hurt, either).

What works best is often a combination of techniques, and different ones at different times. Try some that are new to you, or use them to brainstorm with colleagues. I have yet to meet writing teachers who are immune to grader's block; most everyone has a tip or two to share, and who knows? Your officemate's tip could be the one that works for you.

# Making (Up) the Grade

As an undergraduate, I attended Reed College, where course grades, although assigned, are not reported directly to students. You can ask for your grades, but I never knew anyone who did. When you are already trying your best, a high grade sends the message that you don't need to work so hard, and a low grade is discouraging. In graduate school, at the School for International Training, the classes were all pass/fail.

While those systems were excellent for my own education, they did not prepare me for assigning grades to others and coping with the subsequent reactions. I used to think that every student walked into class with a C (average, right?) and worked up to a B by either expending effort or achieving results, or up to an A through effort combined with results.

Students, on the other hand, assume that they walk in with an A; if they are bad, they are punished with a B, or if they are truly bad, even a C. Some ESL students come from systems where effort and sincerity are rewarded even if results are not always achieved; from that point of view, a low grade casts a negative light on the student's character.

Many students have assumptions I didn't expect: that a grade below an A means some sort of failure, that a less-than-perfect grade point average (GPA) (in some institutions, now well above a 4.0) means one will never get into graduate school, and that grades can be raised if one presses the teacher hard enough.

It could be just my imagination that students challenge grades more each year. Perhaps someone will uncover ancient Greek or Egyptian scriptures from some sage bemoaning the number of pupils contesting an assessment. But every time I pass back papers with grades of B+ or lower, I know I can expect emails and office visits to follow. I've had students burst into tears over Bs, and I've been dragged through Grade Grievance Court over an A-. And while some students ask about extra credit or for the chance to rewrite the paper, others just request a higher grade.

Sometimes students see ESL teachers as an easy touch. ESL classes are often smaller, and the teachers do more oral and small-group work. This makes ESL teachers seem friendlier and more accessible, so students think they have a chance to prevail upon teachers' goodwill or prove their own sincerity. I asked one student who wanted me to raise his final grade of B- so he could avoid academic probation why he wasn't talking to the professors who had given him Ds. "Oh, real professors won't change grades," he told me.

Most teachers have felt the pressure to give higher grades. After all, classes run more smoothly when students are happy, and student evaluations are higher. I've been guilty of inflation, too. Once, when a student came in and demanded without preamble, "Why did this paper get a B?" I was sorely tempted to tell him, "Because it was a solid C paper." It's hard to prove to students why they didn't get As, especially in writing and speaking classes.

Some teachers devise complicated point systems and calculate grades with spreadsheet programs intended to prove as conclusively as possible that the grades assigned are justified. But does assigning higher grades assure smooth sailing for all concerned?

One of my strongest students came to see me just before the end of term to check his grade. Bless his soul, I thought, and he's modest, too. I reminded him that he'd had an A on every assignment, and I explained how he'd also earned an A for intangibles such as participation and effort in class. He was silent a moment. "So, not an A+?"

Because that's the real problem with grade inflation, isn't it? In a town where all the children are above average, there's no way to stand out. Students have no way of knowing how they're doing if only top grades are given out and if they're given to please rather than to assess.

If you must give out grades, they must mean something, and they must be accurate. If you struggle with grading issues, try talking to professors and instructors in other departments. Some departments distribute a list of courses and final grades so that teachers can see whether they are grading in line with their peers. You might also talk with a university academic adviser (or, better yet, have one come in to talk to your class) about what kind of GPAs are considered necessary for graduate school.

Reed College, incidentally, has experienced no grade inflation for the past nineteen years. However, the college is obliged to send out a report with each transcript to explain that to graduate schools so their students can compete successfully with higher GPAs from other institutions (on the college's grading policy, see Reed College, http://web.reed.edu/registrar/transcripts.html; at press time, this page also had a link to the .pdf file that Reed sends to graduate schools explaining the lack of grade inflation).

The absence of the carrot and the stick of grades is not for everyone, nor is it necessarily an available option. But when teachers and students view grades and their values differently, one solution is to discuss the matter openly. If you can explore a cultural or a controversial issue in class, spend a session on grading: What are expectations in different cultures? Is grade inflation a problem? Is it possible (or desirable) for every student in a class to get an A? You may not agree on the answers, but it's an opportunity for each side to see where the other stands.

# Observe This

My office mate, an old timer, was full of concern for me, the new hire. "So, Carol's going to observe your class on Thursday, right? Do you have a lesson plan?"

"Yes, of course." I ran through a brief outline of what I'd planned.

My office mate was silent for a moment. "Oh. You know, Carol likes to see a lot of pair work. You might want to take that into consideration."

"Well, there's some pair work; but I have a lot of information to deliver in a short amount of time, and a mini lecture is the most efficient way to do it."

"I know, but... I just thought you should know that Carol really likes to see a lot of pair work."

Ah, the peer evaluation. Seemingly rare in other departments, it's been a common feature of every university ESL program in which I've taught. There are two main types of peer observation: That used for evaluation, where the observer judges the person observed; or that used for professional development by either the observer or the person observed. The former puts my back up; the latter can be a highly useful helpful tool for improving or revitalizing one's teaching or dealing with issues in a specific class.

Peer observation as evaluation strikes me as unnatural by definition: A "peer" doesn't pass judgment. That's the job of an administrator or director, and I've experienced useful observations from some enlightened and helpful directors. But I've never been comfortable being judged by a colleague or being asked to judge one. It's a situation almost guaranteed to bring up feelings of "You're not the boss of me" in the person observed, and puts the observer in the awkward position of being expected to judge someone often of equal but different talent, style, and experience. Teachers I know have been criticized by peer observers for things like walking around the classroom while teaching ("It might make the students nervous"), moving arms while talking ("It made me uncomfortable"), and asking a student not to copy another student's work in class ("I felt there was some underlying hostility"). Were these glaring faults in the observed teacher's pedagogy, or merely personal differences in teaching style? These would be funny stories if the judgments were not put into the teachers' files and used to inform the overall rating of the teacher's classroom performance.

On the other hand, peer observation as a development tool for either the observer or the person observed can be valuable, if done right. To that end, I offer the following advice:

• The peer observation should be useful to either the observer or the person observed. In a perfect world, it might be useful to both; but I'd settle for it being useful to one. In fact, it should be so useful that the person could express in a clear sentence what she hopes to achieve or learn. (If you think this happens automatically with peer observations, then you haven't asked around.)

A clear goal, by the way, is not "I wonder what Nancy's class is like" or "If I watch Ken for an hour, it counts as 'professional development.' " Rather, a clear goal for an observer would be something like "I'd like to learn how Sue pre-teaches vocabulary for the longer reading passages, and how that works with a large class." An observer can't focus on everything; he needs to choose one or a few areas in which to concentrate.

For the observed teacher too, a specific goal such as "The small group discussions in this class never seem to get off the ground, even though I'm using techniques that have always been successful for me. I hope my observer can give me some insights and suggestions" will yield more observations of value than "Could you see how my writing class is going?"

• The goals for the observation should be discussed before the observation, as well as after. Both the observer and the person observed should know exactly what the point of the observation is.

• During the observation, the observer should observe. That means he should not take part in the class, ask questions, join a small group. If he's participating, he's not paying full attention to everything that's going on.

• Should the observer take notes? That's something to discuss. Some people feel unnerved by the sight of someone writing all through the lesson. If the observer is concentrating on a few specific points, she can probably remember them and write down her impressions just after the class. On the other hand, if the person observed wants to know how many minutes different groups spent on each task, or what vocabulary words they needed to check, taking notes might be necessary.

• After the observation, there should be adequate time allowed to discuss what happened. I like to let the person who taught speak first, and give his impressions of what happened in the class and why. A non-judging observer would then give her impressions, including advice if that was wanted.

What did I do about Carol's observation? Changing the lesson to suit an observer didn't seem fair to the students. Not changing the lesson to suit the observer seemed like it wouldn't earn me a positive evaluation – and this was an evaluation that would "count" towards my year-end rating. I make it sound like I deliberated, though I never actually considered changing my original plan. The observation mostly served to remind me why I don't like peer observation as an evaluation tool. One day in the life of a class is just a snapshot, not a complete view of how the class is going. However, for the right purposes, I would still welcome an observer in my class any time, and I'll continue to observe other teachers when asked and when I want to learn.

# TOEFL Driven

I recently had to renew my U.S. driver's license, which I knew would involve taking the thirty-item multiple-choice "knowledge" test. Now, I've been driving for most of my adult life. I believe I drive well: I'm calm, patient, and polite; I drive defensively; I'm aware of my surroundings; I know the rules of the road; I've never gotten a traffic ticket. In short, I have communicative competence in driving.

And yet I knew better than to walk in and try to pass that knowledge test without having studied the official state driving booklet full of information on, for example, how far away from railroad tracks you must stop if there is no marking on the pavement (fifteen feet) and what the speed limit is in an unmarked commercial district (twenty-five miles per hour). Nor did I choose to study gradually over several weeks, reviewing a few rules each day. No, I read the whole thing a few days before the test and then skimmed though it the morning of the test.

As I was taking the test, it struck me that I had prepared for it in much the same way many students wish to prepare for the Test of English as a Foreign Language (TOEFL). That is, even though speaking, listening to, reading, and writing English at a college or university – the "driving" – are what they intend to do, they know that they can't do it until they pass that knowledge test.

We ESL teachers get frustrated with students who tell us that they want to study for the TOEFL rather than learn English (especially when they state it so baldly). Yet we can't deny the power that the test has over their academic lives. If they handled English wonderfully but didn't pass the test, most institutions of higher education would deny them admission.

The frustration arises because teachers know that passing the test alone is not enough. If you passed the knowledge test for a driver's license but not the practical driving test, you wouldn't get a license. But in the academic world, students can often pass the knowledge test and then be set adrift in classes for which they haven't been truly prepared. Of what use is it, then, to achieve a passing TOEFL score if they are going to struggle miserably in or even fail at their academic classes?

The concept is clear to teachers. But have you ever tried to get it across to a class of students? I must have spent years lecturing students about how useful solid academic English classes would be for their future academic lives and explaining how passing the TOEFL was just the beginning of their language challenges and not the end. "Don't study for the TOEFL!" I would cry. "Study English! And the TOEFL will take care of itself."

Naturally, and rightly, these lectures have never changed anyone's mind. In truth, sometimes I felt so frustrated with students' focus on the TOEFL that I tried too hard to swing them the other way and didn't pay as much attention to the test as I should have. You could, after all, be quite skilled in steering and maneuvering a car, but if you didn't know who has the right of way when four cars come to a four-way intersection at the same time, there could be serious consequences.

I see two solutions. The most important is at the organizational level. If your program offers TOEFL classes (and I think it should), then they should be offered only to students who have already taken classes or demonstrated proficiency in other key skills, such as academic writing, speaking, understanding the U.S. university culture, or whatever skills your institution has found to be necessary. Before they have their TOEFL scores, the students are your captive audience.

Of course, some institutions will matriculate students with too low a TOEFL score. This makes financial sense, because students with the lower scores will apply to institutions that will accept them. But if you work for one of those institutions, lobby hard to have students with a "passing" but still low score take the ESL program's placement test anyway. (It helps if the classes you offer to matriculated students are credit-bearing, but that's another story for another column.)

The second, and for many the more practicable, solution is to let the TOEFL fever drive your classes. Offer a course in TOEFL English, since that's what students want, and then use that course to teach vocabulary, grammar, reading, listening, writing, and, yes, test-taking strategies.

Techniques that worked for my driver's license knowledge test also work for many students: I studied the information (and reviewed the more obscure rules just before the test), I learned how it would be tested, I took practice tests online, I talked to others who had taken the test before, and I got a good night's rest and ate a decent breakfast before the test (and I passed, with a 97).

Just being familiar with computerized multiple-choice tests helped me breeze through the test more quickly than the people around me, several of whom looked distinctly nervous. Certainly children in K–12 schools are given practice tests to become familiar with the content and format before taking their increasingly high-stakes standardized tests.

Even if you can't offer a course with such an enticing title, simply pointing out that "being able to write a strong, clear topic sentence will help you get a higher score on the TOEFL" will perk your students right up.

Teaching *for* the test is not the same as teaching *to* the test. The TOEFL is neither evil nor irrelevant; it covers the same English language you teach in class, even if it tests in a multiple choice format. Giving students a solid foundation in English and then helping them feel familiar and comfortable with a standardized test should prepare them for both the TOEFL and the academic world beyond.

# Are End-of-Term Evaluations Already Too Late?

As students get into classes that increasingly "count" in terms of grades and credits, the end-of-term class party is increasingly displaced by end-of-term evaluations (except in classes that first have a party and then pass out evaluations – which, I've heard, helps one's overall class rating, though I've never tried it).

Every intensive English and university program I've taught in has required teachers to give out and collect end-of-term evaluations, both bubble forms and blank sheets for additional comments. The bubble forms produce the statistics that your department may (or may not) use for evidence of the quality of your teaching. Every ESL class I've taught in the United States has had fewer students than would make up a statistically significant – or even somewhat accurate – sample size, but that never seems to have given a department pause.

The comment sheets, which may be signed or unsigned, are supposed to give you insights that standardized questions cannot. At one university where I taught, you could choose whether to include comment sheets in your teaching portfolio, but only if they were signed. Another university required comment sheets to be included if they were signed and forbade them if they weren't.

Comments typically range from pointless ("I wish

the bending machines to have sprit not just coke") to obscure ("I thank my English") to revealing (from my
French 101 class: "You tried to teach us too much French
– that's not why we're here") all the way to useful ("I
think we need more practice paraphrasing as whole
class, not just groups or partners").

One reason not all comments are useful is that many
ESL students aren't used to evaluating courses and
teachers, and don't know what they're supposed to
write. Is the comment sheet a suggestion box? A way to
thank their teachers? The few lines of instructions at the
top of the page are probably not enough to make this
clear.

It's worth spending five or ten minutes of class time
explaining to students why they're being asked for their
opinions, how their comments will be used, and what
sorts of comments are useful. For example, while not a
morning person, I've somehow always ended up with
classes that start at 8:00 a.m., which are clearly not a favorite of students either. However, the class time is definitely not negotiable. Making this clear to a class of
twenty-five students means that I'll get only four or five
comments about changing the class time instead of twen-
ty-three.

But the real problem with comments is that they
come at a point in the term when you can't do anything
about them. In the fall, the listening/speaking class
wants more authentic listening activities. So you change
your syllabus for the spring term, only to have the new
class complain in May that there were too many listening
activities and not enough opportunities for conversation.

The best solution I've experienced is the SGID, or *small-group instructional diagnosis*, a technique for midterm classroom evaluation that has been around in various forms since the 1970s. In the version I've used, you arrange to swap classrooms for one class period with a fellow teacher around midterm. In advance, you prepare a sheet of questions for your students about how the class is going. A helpful Web site from the University of Washington (2005) even gives you sample question sheets, but you'll probably want to write your own.

The cooperating teacher takes over your class for the period and leads the class through the process. The teacher distributes the sheets to the class, which they discuss in small groups without needing to reach any kind of consensus.

Students are not only allowed but encouraged to speak in their native language. I've done this several times with classes that included several core groups speaking one language or another and a few isolated speakers of other languages; those students formed a group on their own and used English, and it was never a problem.

When the discussions are done, the cooperating teacher writes categories such as *Going well, Not going well, Suggestions* on the board, a projector, or a sheet of butcher paper, and solicits responses from everyone in the class. When several students agree, the teacher can just tally responses.

Since the students watch the teacher write, they can make sure their ideas are reported accurately. All dissenting opinions are written down, even if there is a clear majority. No names are used.

When the class is over, you and the cooperating teacher meet and go over the feedback. You then discuss your response with the class at the next session.

Here are the advantages of SGID:

• Students hear from all others in the class and realize that others share – or don't share – their feelings.

• Students are more likely to report minor concerns that they might not bother mentioning on an end-of-term form from the university.

• You have a chance to explain why you cannot make some changes they've requested and to explain the purpose of some unpopular activities.

• You have a chance to make reasonable changes.

This last advantage is the most important, I think – it shows students that you are listening, do care, and are flexible. And the evaluation happens while the students are still in class, so the changes you make affect the people who have asked for them. A student once requested that I write up the class calendar (in outline form on the syllabus) in calendar form. The change was easy to make, and I handed her a calendar-style schedule at the next class. She would never have scheduled an office visit to request this or mentioned it as a criticism on a final evaluation, but my change made her life easier, and she was touchingly grateful that I did it.

Although a class period and a half may seem like a lot of time to spend on a class evaluation, I've always found it worthwhile. The second half of your class will go more smoothly, and, as a bonus, your end-of-term evaluations will probably be higher, too.

**Reference**

University of Washington, Center for Instructional Development and Research. (2005). Midterm class interviews.
http://depts.washington.edu/cidrweb/SGID.html.

# Middle School Memories

I've spent most of my teaching life in university classrooms. However, in search of a job with health insurance, I once spent a year in a private secondary school, armed with only dim memories of my own school days and some helpful suggestions from colleagues ("Remember – they can smell your fear"). After all, I reasoned, how hard could it be? ESL is ESL. These students would be just the same as the others, only shorter.

It was . . . different. I taught the lowest level classes, so the students came in with almost no English. Fortunately, they were young, flexible, and living in an English-speaking country, and within just days they were confidently calling out their first English phrase: "Extra credit!"

(What *is* it with extra credit? Students would ask about it before even beginning the regular assignment, and would work harder and longer on something with that magic label. If I had to do it all over again, I'd just call everything extra credit.)

The contact hours were higher than at the university, the classes were larger, and the students had twice as much energy and three times as many questions, many of which had nothing to do with ESL. It was an exhilarating (if exhausting) ride, but at the time I had trouble making sense of it all. Each class period seemed like an episode in a situation comedy in which I played the bumbling title role.

Last fall, my own child started middle school, and the memories came flooding back. And I realized that enough time has passed for me to recognize the lessons presented to me in such memorable episodes as these:

**The feminine protection episode:** Just before class, Marina frantically beckoned me outside. As soon as I stepped out, she pulled me to the side and whipped a tampon out of her pocket. "I have to know how to use this before third period," she said. "For PE [physical education] class. Swimming. In America, it isn't excuse." Her mother, it appeared, didn't know how to use one either and had sent her off with inadequate instructions. I'd never actually read a job description for my position, but I was sure this wasn't in it.

In my cowardice, I attempted to pass the buck: "Why don't you ask your PE teacher?"

Marina blushed. "I'm too embarrassed to ask him."

Fortunately, we had just been studying giving instructions and had even talked about the value of a diagram, which I hastily drew. I never asked for a progress report, but Marina passed PE, including swimming.

**The unfortunate nickname episode:** In grammar class, students were taking turns reading aloud from a textbook some sentences they'd put into the simple past. One by one, they read sentences in which various characters – Mary, Bob, Sandy, and so on – performed their simple past actions.

Things went smoothly until little Kazu read out sentence 6: "Dick ____ his apartment in a hurry this morning because he was late for school."

Pandemonium.

"Ms. Zemach! Did you hear what he said?"

"Is he going to get detention?"

"Read it again, Kazu!"

"Is that really someone's name? It's not against the law?"

In his embarrassment, Kazu actually slipped through the back of his seat, wedging in his rear end and leaving his arms and legs flailing in the air in front of him. It took me and a husky Tongan boy several minutes of tugging to extract him. No more grammar was checked during that class.

**The squashed bug episode:** Our ground-floor classroom, whose door to the outside I left open for ventilation, attracted a number of slow-moving beetles. The boys used to step on them until I threatened the loss of five points on a quiz to any killers. Instead, I explained, bugs that entered my classroom were sent back outside.

One day, as I carefully swept another beetle outside, the art teacher walked by outside and squashed the beetle flat in front of the class, to the students' vast delight.

"Are you going to take five points off *her* quiz, Ms. Zemach?"

**The minimal pairs episode:** Kenta's favorite English phrase was "No fair!", which he used liberally and often. I'd announce a quiz the next week: "No fair!" Some homework for that evening: "No fair!" A multidisciplinary project: "No fair!" Some group work: "No fair!" Ignoring it, challenging it, and questioning it did nothing to discourage him.

Finally I used the five-points threat, which worked. But he stayed after class shortly afterwards to ask me what was wrong with saying "No fair." I told him using the phrase was whining – blaming someone else for his own failure to take responsibility.

He looked confused. "But then why is it OK for Americans to wear it on their shirts?" (Our school's dress code forbade offensive language on shirts.)

"I don't think anyone has that on a shirt."

"They do, lots of them," he insisted. He pointed to an older boy walking by outside. "See the back of his shirt?"

In large letters, it said "No fear" – the brand name and slogan of a popular clothing company that sold surfing gear. Here was a teaching moment in both pronunciation and attitude, and after five minutes of drilling, I gave Kenta permission to say "No fear!" when I announced an assignment.

Here are the lessons I learned from these episodes:

• Expect the unexpected. You may be (or seem to be) the only resource the students have.

• If you're writing a worksheet (or a textbook), and you must use a short name in order to save space, try Rick or Nick or Vic. But not that other one.

• The threat of losing points on a future quiz is a pretty good tool for behavior modification. However, you can only control your own classroom, not the world outside.

• Things aren't always what they seem. Before you assume a student has an attitude problem, take the time to talk with him or her.

And never forget the power of extra credit.

# English Only?

When I tell people that I teach English to students who speak a different native language, the first response is invariably, "Wow, how many languages do you have to speak?" I explain that I actually don't need to speak the native languages of each of my students, because in class we all speak only English. The other person usually looks dubious here, and may even mutter, "I don't see how that could work." And, of course, it often doesn't work like that. If two students in one class share a native language, they're probably going to use it at times – or at least, wish they could.

So what? What's the harm? The reasons against letting students use their native language in class are many. It wastes time. It distracts other students. It excludes students who do not understand that language. It increases a teacher's paranoia (*Are* they talking about you? Well – have you ever discussed students with another teacher?). It decreases the opportunities for those students to practice speaking and listening to English.

Some teachers are more concerned about these dangers than others. I taught in a program once where one of the teachers patrolled the areas outside the classrooms during the breaks between classes and actually shot students speaking their native languages with a water pistol. While I felt that attacking students might be going a bit far, I did develop my own methods for keeping students in English. For example, I'd put one mark on the chalkboard each time someone spoke a native language, and when the class earned more than 10 marks, I gave the entire class extra homework (that way, students police each other); or I charged students 100 yen (or 25 cents, or whatever was appropriate for where I was teaching) each time they spoke a language other than English, and at the end of the term we used the money to finance a class party.

Of course, even in my earlier days, I recognized the value of sometimes using the native language to help teach English. It is a far more efficient use of class time to let a low-level student ask, "How do you say *bengoshi* in English?" than to try to explain or mime *lawyer*. However, I did feel that the use of one's native language should be limited at best, and of course should be used only for asking about English.

My feeling changed when I taught for a year at a language center in Morocco. The center offered its foreign teachers free Arabic lessons, so I enrolled in a beginning class. The teacher, who spoke fluent French and reasonable English, insisted that only Arabic be used in class. Unfortunately, she was not a very good teacher, and after about three lessons, everyone was lost. She'd say something and fix us with a piercing stare, and we'd have no idea what to do. Should we repeat what she'd said? Was it a question we were supposed to answer? We cared about doing the right thing because she had the disconcerting habit of laughing loudly at our mistakes and yelling what we thought were probably insults at us (we didn't know, of course, but they sure didn't sound like compliments or commiserations). There was one woman in the class who had a Moroccan husband

and knew a little Arabic, so if the teacher's back was turned we'd frantically whisper, "Angie – do we have to write this down? What page are we supposed to be on? Who has to go to the board next?" But the teacher was usually too quick for us, and Angie refused to try to help us after a few lessons because she was tired of being yelled at.

I sat next to a friendly Canadian man. We shared English, French, and the same sense of humor; and while we were both serious language learners, a lot of things in class struck us as funny, and we would sometimes whisper remarks to each other or pass notes. The teacher was furious, and reported us both to the director as "bad students." After that, we both dropped the class, followed soon by the rest of the students.

While I never learned much Arabic, I did learn some other reasons to speak one's native language in class: to make friends and to have a good time. I learn better when I'm enjoying myself, and I'm sure I'm not alone in this. After my year in Morocco, I eased up remarkably on my former "English only" policy, to the point where I once allowed an advanced academic writing class with only Thai students to speak in Thai whenever they felt they needed to, as long as they were on task. It was scary at first – I felt like I was breaking some sort of rule, and worried that the students might tell others and that I would somehow get in trouble. One thing I didn't worry about was keeping students on task, because I found I could easily tell when they had switched from discussing writing to just chatting, even though I don't speak a word of Thai. A good bit of Thai was used during peer reviews, but the students made progress in English and their writing improved; and they enjoyed the class and found it useful.

All that not to say that things can't get out of hand. There have been times when, had someone handed me a water pistol, I might not have been able to promise that some students wouldn't get wet. So the next to last thing I would like to share is my favorite way to keep a class in English, when necessary.

When I taught at Sumitomo Electric Industries in Japan, we had a two-week intensive immersion program every year for 24 incoming workers. Though the students generally had quite low levels of English, they were supposed to stay entirely in English for the whole two weeks, including break times, meal times, and rest times. The method for enforcing this was to give each student 10 large safety pins, called "boo-boo pins" (this name, of course, is not essential), which they kept with them at all times. If a student spoke Japanese, a trainer or any other student could take the offender's pin and add it to his or her own collection. In the two weeks, a student rarely lost more than four or five pins. It was an amazing technique, and while I can't explain exactly why it works so well, I've had similar success with it in the US using paper clips (different colors for each student is a nice touch).

In closing, I'll ask you to consider your policy on English in the classroom. Whether you've been teaching three months or 30 years, you doubtless have one, even if you have never articulated it. Ask yourself too what beliefs your policy reflects. Please don't go so far as to carry a loaded (water) gun, but do consider whether your policy is working for both you and your students, or whether you'd like to either ease up or tighten the reins.

# Teacher Burnout Part 1:
# Burnout from Teaching

As you read the following profiles of two former colleagues, identify the teacher suffering from burnout.

To explain why she became a teacher, **Amanda** said, "Because I love being in the classroom. I just love helping people." And she does. Amanda is always there for her students, even outside scheduled office hours.

Students have her email address and home telephone number, and they know she responds on weekends. She's saved every class photo, every gift, and even projects and papers from former students.

She's there for the program and her colleagues, too. She never misses a faculty meeting and volunteers for projects and committees. She's at every placement and testing session; she's even been known to get up at 5:00 a.m. to bake gingerbread for posttest grading sessions.

**Zoe**, on the other hand, sees her students in class and during office hours, but her office door is closed at other times. Her home telephone number is unlisted, and she doesn't answer emails on weekends. Student photos are emptied into the trash at the end of each term, and gifts are discarded at thrift stores. Zoe serves on committees when required, though she insists on email communications instead of meetings whenever possible. She doesn't bake anything for required meetings but might pick up something at the store.

How did I know one of these teachers was suffering from burnout in the first place? Well, she started crying unexpectedly at faculty meetings, escalated to weeping in the halls, and finally quit teaching altogether; whereas Zoe is happily continuing in her sixteenth year of ESL teaching, popular with both students and colleagues.

Psychologist Herbert Freudenberger first coined the term burnout in his 1974 book, *Burnout: The High Cost of High Achievement*, defining it as a state of physical and emotional depletion resulting from conditions of work. Long laundry lists of burnout symptoms can be found all over the Internet: fatigue or exhaustion; decreased motivation and efficiency; anxiety and depression; headaches; insomnia; a sense of helplessness, hopelessness, or worthlessness; a sense of unending stress; and so on. Victims of burnout may either leave the profession or, worse, endure for years, suffering mental, emotional, and physical damage.

In ESL, burnout is triggered by the work of teaching, poor job conditions, or both.

This column discusses burnout from work; I'll talk about burnout from job conditions in a subsequent column. Teaching leads to burnout because

- It attracts personalities drawn to burnout.
- Most teachers work in isolation.

• The classroom interaction can be emotionally draining.

• There are physical demands.

• There is often a lack of emotional support from colleagues and supervisors.

The Indiana University East's Beginning Teacher Mentor Program describes two main burnout-prone personality types.

The *overly conscientious type* is moral and dedicated, with a strong desire to help. However, excessive empathy and overly high self-expectations lead this person to give too much to others, often to compensate for hidden feelings of inadequacy.

The *guilt-motivated type* feels overly responsible for other people and feels the need to continuously give in order to make up for something. Both types deny their own feelings, have a strong need for approval, need to feel indispensable, and have trouble setting appropriate limits and expectations. They may also feel that they are the only ones capable of doing the work properly and may substitute work for elements missing in their personal lives.

Unfortunately, the classroom is a poor place to meet these needs. Most teachers teach alone and for the most part unnoticed. In many U.S. institutions, the ESL programs themselves are isolated on the fringes of campus and given the oldest offices and the smallest classrooms. People don't think of teaching as an isolating profession because, after all, there are classrooms full of students. However, students are not peers or friends. Teachers may like students and be friendly to them – but they are not friends. However, in a situation where students may be the only people teachers interact with over the course of several days, they risk seeing students as people from whom to seek approval, support, and friendship.

The nature of classroom interaction can lead to a blurring of the boundaries of healthy student-teacher relationships. Teachers in English-speaking countries may be the only resource students have, so they find themselves helping students with matters other than English. We hear about students' traffic tickets, their visa troubles, their roommate problems, their parents' pressure to start taking "real" classes next term, or their worry that they'll have to go home and join the army. These are things the economics professor doesn't hear about. For teachers in non-English-speaking countries, students may be the only people they meet for months with whom they can communicate. To practice English and communication, teachers participate in discussions of moral and ethical issues, values, and life experiences. But teachers need to maintain their roles in the classroom. A teacher supports and encourages, but also corrects and assesses. You can't give your friend a C.

People also don't think of teaching as a physically demanding activity, and most teachers I know haven't built up large muscles from hefting books. But I know plenty of teachers with weight problems – they're underweight from skipping meals, or they're overweight from overloading on sugary or fatty foods to keep their energy and moods perpetually up for the classroom stage. Poor eating and sleeping habits lead to more health problems. Simply put, a physically demanding job is not just one that makes you sweat, but one that stresses your body.

What reward do teachers get for coping with this stress? When salaries and working conditions are not rewarding, they need at least verbal recognition and praise. However, many programs aren't configured to allow that. Supervisors and colleagues are more alert to problems.

Popular teachers who handle challenges well may be "rewarded" with larger classes and more of them, while less successful ones get release time for other projects. Thus, less able teachers ironically may get more support and career development opportunities; more capable teachers must seek out professional growth opportunities on their own, while still teaching a full load.

Most teachers are probably more Amanda than Zoe. But there are solutions to burnout from work. For mine, see the next essay "Recharge, Reduce, Reconnect, Recycle," reprinted from the online Compleat Links column that appeared in September 2006 on the TESOL website.

**Reference**

Freudenberger, H. (1974). *Burnout: The high cost of high achievement*. New York: Bantam Books.

# Recharge, Reduce, Reconnect, Recycle

The nature of teaching as a profession can lead to burnout, especially in the types of people commonly drawn to teaching. However, there are solutions to problems related to teacher burnout. While it may not be possible (or desirable) to change your personality, and you cannot change what it means to be a teacher, you can change your behaviors and your reactions to situations.

## Recharge

The most important as well as the most obvious solution is to take care of yourself first. When you fly, there's a reason that the flight attendant tells you that, in the event of an unexpected loss of cabin pressure, to fix your own oxygen mask before you help your children. In the same way, you will not be of much use to your students (or anyone else) if you're exhausted and unhealthy. This means that sometimes you have to say no: no to giving students access to you 24/7, no to correcting their essays two years after they've left your class, no to extra committee assignments, and no to waking up at 5:00 a.m. to bake gingerbread for the faculty meeting.

As well as decent food (so say no to schedules that don't leave you time for meals) and enough sleep, you need regular exercise and a method of relaxation. I don't think it matters whether you meditate, pray, take long walks, or read novels in a bubble bath, but you need something. Sleeping does not count as relaxation, either.

Just remind yourself that you need a method for relaxation far more than you need another coursebook or workshop.

## Reduce

If you're overworked and your institution can't or won't reduce your workload, you need to do it yourself. Figure out what the most stressful parts of your teaching life are, and find solutions.

A good rule of thumb is that it shouldn't take you longer to prepare your lesson than to teach it, and far less time once you've taught it over several terms. Your students won't face disaster if they write two drafts instead of three, or one paper per term instead of two. If you don't have time to read and respond to dialogue journals, have students write to each other, or to keypals, or just to themselves. If you can't handle thirty book reports, have students present them orally; in groups, even, using peer assessment. Sure, students might love it when you show them episodes of Friends for which you've laboriously transcribed every word; but if that takes you all weekend, maybe you need to ask yourself if it's really worth that kind of effort.

An important point here is that when you see your colleagues taking steps to cut back, be supportive. A colleague who's found an easier or more efficient way to do things is not a slacker. Some institutions encourage a pride in workaholism; you don't want to be a winner in any competition to suffer the most. I once overheard a colleague say of another, "Her problem is that she doesn't work any harder than she has to." The second colleague, of course, knew enough to take that as a compliment – but it wasn't meant as one.

Meetings should be arranged to deal with as few administrative matters as possible and to allow more time for teachers to share their methods in order to reconnect, save time, and renew their energy.

## Reconnect

Build a professional support network. This is especially important for teachers who work alone or in small institutions, but anyone can benefit from reaching out to like-minded colleagues. If you're having a problem at work, sometimes it's healthier, as well as easier, to discuss it with someone who has no direct connections to your institution.

Join your TESOL interest section's e-list, for example, or connect to other teachers on Facebook. Stay in touch with people you meet at conferences. Make friends with teachers in other disciplines. These people can be the ones to offer you praise and encouragement, and they can offer you solutions for problems when you're feeling stuck. It's also important to have friends outside of work, of course, but they're of limited help when it comes to brainstorming solutions to your work crises. The point is, if you have enough people to help you with your work life, you won't need to drag your family and friends into problems at work.

## Recycle

Collaborate at work. Plan lessons together. Share worksheets. Yes, I've worked at places where teachers didn't want to collaborate – but more often at institutions that hadn't even thought of how to encourage collaboration, let alone acted to facilitate it. Even when teaching different sections of the same class, sometimes teachers won't use the same worksheets because they don't have an easy way to share. Create a binder, put a clean copy of any good worksheet in a plastic sheet protector, and then anyone can photocopy it. A worksheet is no less "good" because your coworker wrote it. Try not to create worksheets that cannot be used for more than one term. Look for textbooks that truly fit your class so that you don't have to create too many worksheets in the first place.

## Don't Label Colleagues "Burned Out"

My final word on burnout here is to not overuse the term. There's a danger in thinking of yourself as being 'burned out' because you're having an off week, or even an off term. There's even more of a danger in labeling others 'burned out' when they refuse to take on extra assignments or when they don't agree with you or the administration. Teaching is a flexible and people-created profession, and it's up to all of us to create an environment that's healthy for all teachers.

# Teacher Burnout Part 2:
# "Not in it for the Money"

*(Note: the salary figures offered in this column are from 2006. I'd like to think they've crept up a bit. I certainly hope so.)*

Emily, a graduate student in special education, was having problems with her hot water heater again. Two plumbers had failed, so her landlord had come over to work on it himself. "I feel bad for him," said Emily, "because he's in law school and really busy." To cheer her up, I replied, "Well, you don't have to feel *too* sorry for him. He already owns rental property, and when he gets out of school, he'll be a lawyer. Whereas when you graduate, you'll still be renting from him." She laughed. "True. But after all, I'm not going into teaching for the money."

If I had a dollar for every teacher I'd heard make that remark, I could buy private health insurance for three of them. Emily caught me at the wrong (or right?) time, and I questioned her about her attitude. Did she believe that she would be of value to anyone once she started working? Did she think her job was important? How much did she think she ought to be paid when she graduated? How about in ten years? Should she be paid less if she enjoyed her career? More if she didn't enjoy it? Should she be earning as much as her fiancé, a computer engineer? Should he also have a low salary, given that he enjoyed his profession?

In my *Teacher Burnout Part 1* column, I discussed how the nature of teaching can lead to burnout: Its demands are rigorous, and many who choose the profession are prone to overwork and self-sacrifice. However, another leading cause of burnout is poor working conditions such as low salaries, lack of health insurance and retirement benefits, no sick leave, and temporary contracts.

Emily asked what a typical salary for an ESL teacher was. I would happily have told her – if I'd known. Most jobs advertise salaries that are "commensurate with experience" or "competitive" (but with what?). Americans don't typically talk about salaries. It's rude to ask someone what he makes, and strange to tell. So we take whatever's offered because we don't know if it's good or bad, and we've never thought about what we're worth. I can easily count over ten experienced, competent ESL teachers in my circle of acquaintances, working in U.S. institutions of higher learning, who earn less than $30,000 a year, and some less than $25,000.

At least my friend who makes $22,300 has health insurance, which is not the case for many. Some institutions can deny coverage to employees whose contracts are less than a year long or specify less than 40 hours of work a week. I taught for four years (20 contact hours per week) at the University of Hawaii, on consecutive 10-week contracts, with no benefits. I was young, ate well, exercised, and felt lucky. But that's not enough in a country with no national health insurance. The worst that happened was a broken nose, which more or less healed on its own (check my photo – see that little bump?). A colleague was not so lucky – she died, at age 47, after 15 years of full-time teaching, of complications from the diabetes she couldn't afford to treat.

ESL programs are the only ones I know that require sick teachers to find substitutes for their own classes. When a business professor is sick, the department secretary hangs a note on his classroom door canceling the class. ESL teachers, on the other hand, are telephoning their colleagues and frantically typing up lesson plans. Some programs even require teachers to pay their own substitutes in cash. No wonder teachers prefer to teach class while ill.

While most American university professors teach a full course load of anywhere from 8 to 15 weekly contact hours, ESL teachers are called "part time" if they teach, say, 25 hours a week. In order to earn enough money, they teach "part time" at several institutions. Naturally, none of these positions then offer benefits. Many university labor unions don't include part-time faculty, so it's hard to legally address the issue.

While these problems are pervasive and serious, they're also problems that can be solved. Laws are passed and programs are staffed by people, and both can change. Here, then, are some specific recommendations:

1) **Share and research information about salaries.** Talk to teachers of other subjects and ask what they get paid (or look it up – salaries of state employees, including university faculty, are public record). Only post job ads that state the salary range.

2) **Talk to administrators about salaries and benefits.** David Kent shared this story in an email: "I was once in a group of instructors who met with the relevant university vice-president on matters of pay and benefits. When the point was made that full-time people were having to teach part-time at various other institutions to make ends meet, he said that he had assumed that was the way ESL people liked to do things. He said with apparent honesty that he thought ESL people were academic vagabonds (his term), so he had not been concerned with employment practices for us. (To his credit, he apologized and had the program restructured.)"

3) **Write letters to organizations** such as AAIEP (American Association of Intensive English Programs) and CEA (Commission on English Language Program Accreditation) that promote standards for programs and that accredit institutions, and ask that they state a minimum acceptable salary of $30,000. Currently, the CEA posts no criteria related to faculty salaries or benefits – though they do require that *students* have health insurance; and the AAIEP says that faculty must "receive an appropriate salary and fringe benefits" and that "Salaries and benefits for IEP faculty [must be] on a par with those offered by other IEPs in the same geographic region." The teachers I know working for under $25,000 a year work at an institution endorsed by the AAIEP.

4) **Don't take jobs with unacceptable working conditions.** Other professors are paid higher salaries because otherwise, they wouldn't teach – they'd go out and work in private industry. We as a profession have to start refusing salaries that are ridiculous. Is a rotten job really better than no job? Will you still feel that way when you're older?

5) **If you have good working conditions, agitate for those who don't**. It's hard to get politically involved when you're burned out from three jobs. TESOL's active Caucus on Part-time Employment Concerns (COPTEC) is an excellent place to start, and free to join. They deal with the problems and rights of adjunct and temporary employees as well as true part-timers.

Whether you're burned out or not, you have steps to take, either to cure yourself or to prevent burnout down the road; or to help other teachers. Strong teachers make a strong profession, and when one of us burns out, it hurts all of us.

# The Process of Learning Process Writing

Every writing teacher I've ever worked with has taught process writing. However, to English language learners encountering it for the first time, it can seem a sort of cruel joke, if not outright punishment. "We have to do *what* before we write? My paper's going to be checked by the person next to me? What does he know? And then I have to write it *again*?"

It would be hard to pick up a current ESL writing textbook that did not begin with an explanation (and, usually, a justification) of process writing; that is, a method that takes the writer through a series of steps:

- brainstorming, to gather ideas
- organizing, to choose which ideas to use and put them in order
- drafting, to write the complete essay from start to finish
- reviewing, whether by oneself, peers, or the teacher
- editing and revising
- rewriting

Process writing is obviously more time-consuming than simply writing an essay in a single draft and turning it in. But if process writing is so time-consuming and painful for students, why take them through all those steps?

Because it results in better writing, and, eventually, better writers. One term, I decided to have students write their reactions in their journals to stages of the writing process they had not encountered before. Their comments show their understanding of the value of the process.

**Brainstorming:** For this opening stage of the writing process, my classes try discussion, freewriting, listing, and mapping. Brainstorming is usually the most popular part of the process because it's not very difficult. What I want students to learn, though, is which technique works best for them.

*By doing free writing, I can recognize what my English expression is. I can think over it, then other expressions come out. This action is really good because freewriting yield something new that I've never thought. In that time, I am happy and feel my skill developing.*

*Listing is good for me. I have to think a little bit to come up with my idea but I wrote many ideas and this skill made me having less unnecessary stuffs than free writing.*

*If I make a list or freewriting, I don't need to think about the structure and connection at first, I can concentrate on writing down my idea. So when I have to write a large amount quickly, those methods are good. But if I have a lot of time, I surely use mapping because I want to make my sentences much better and deeper. I can instantly understand structure and connection of the contents. It also helps us to see the things from a lot of different aspect, both from inside and outside.*

Students use different methods to gather more ideas, to generate ideas quickly, and to start making logical connections between those ideas – which leads to the next step.

**Organizing:** After they have looked over their ideas, crossed out the unworthy ones, and highlighted the useful ones, students prepare an outline.

*"Outlining" is very useful for organizing the essay. It really help preventing from being disordered. I write the essential sentence on "Outline" and after that, I just add the detailed sentence on "Outline." That's good.*

It can be a hard sell at first, but this student came around in the end:

*October 20: It is also different between the writing in my language and America. We do not have to write the outline because it wastes a lot of time for the writing in my paper.*

*November 27: From what I learned this term, the most important thing I learn is the outline because it save a lot of time on the writing and good organization.*

**Peer editing:** I believe that, especially for low-level writers, peer editing has a greater value to the reader than to the writer. I provide readers with a detailed form to fill out, asking them to locate topic sentences, examples of support, strong language, and so on; and I grade the readers, not the writers, on the form. That said, writers benefit from knowing that they can communicate and that their work is appreciated. I do not ask peers to check grammar or spelling; that's the instructor's job.

*It is so interested to me to read other people's essay because it is always different from mine. This time, I read Sachiko's paper and she wrote about nature and nurture. She explains them so logically.*

*First draft of essay was much easier for me to write than before. We had some steps to finish the paper and when I done this step each by each, I did not need to think about anything just write the essay with brainstorming and outline that I made before. However, later I read it and show someone to read, I recognized where I should fix.*

Here the writer mentions being able to see for herself what she should change, just from having shown her paper to someone else; in fact, one advantage of process writing is precisely that it takes time.

*I couldn't find any mistakes in my papers soon after writing them, but I can find many mistakes now. I don't exactly know why, but it makes writings better to review papers after taking them away for a while.*

If you teach process writing, begin by explaining in advance the nature and purpose of each step. Be clear with yourself as well as your students: Will you require two drafts? Three? Will you mark papers before you give a grade? Will peer edits "count" towards anyone's final grade? Will you grade process as well as product? How? I don't think the answers to these questions matter, as long as you know what you're doing and why, and can articulate it.

If your students keep writing journals, consider having them chart their thoughts at each stage of their first essay; then have them go back and reread their comments before they start their second paper. In this way, you'll be nurturing thoughtful writers, such as this one:

*At the beginning of the class, I think I know what is writing, but I find it is wrong. Writing is not a easy task. From brainstorm to final draft, there is many process you need to pay attention. Through all the journal entries, I learned how to produce a essay, what step I need to do, how can I get the idea. After this term, I have changed my mind. Writing is not a trick, I need to do it seriously.*

# Picture This

The first house we bought came with a stove with four burners, two in front and two in back. There were, naturally, four knobs on the stove, one to turn on and off each burner, and they were labeled to indicate which knob controlled which burner: *left front*, *left back*, *right front*, and *right back*. Pretty simple – and yet, from time to time, my native English-speaking husband would burn a pot or not cook something because he had turned on the wrong burner.

Then we bought a new stove. This one had four knobs for the four burners, but they weren't labeled with words – instead, each knob showed a diagram of a square (the stove top) with one little circle (a burner) in each corner. One circle in each square was filled in, to indicate the position of the burner it corresponded to. Well, my husband never burned another pot – but I started to.

Better than any lecture or article, the two stoves proved to me that there really is a difference between visual learners, like my artist husband, and verbal learners, like me. Visual learners process information most easily when they can see it as a picture, diagram, or live-action scene in a movie or play. Verbal learners learn better from lectures or reading.

A speaker I heard once at a JALT (Japan Association of Language Teachers) conference asserted that more people are visual learners than are verbal learners – but that verbal learners are more likely to become language teachers and textbook writers. Accurate figures are hard to come by, and if there is a definitive statistic out there giving percentages in any population of visual learners and verbal learners, I haven't seen it (possibly it exists only as a visual or a chart, and I just didn't understand it). I can imagine carrying out such a study: I would ask a group of students to approach two stoves, one labeled with words and one labeled with a diagram, and time how long it took them to turn on the burner under the kettle and boil water for tea. But who has time to carry out a study like that? And what teacher can afford two stoves?

But I do know that my ESL classes are filled with students who are visual learners. They make word maps to brainstorm for their essays (I'd write a list). They spend time looking at the photos and diagrams in their textbooks (I'd skip straight to the exercises). They were relieved when Macintosh computers began using more symbols and fewer words to label folders and applications, which continues to be an irritation to me.

So what does a verbal teacher do to relate material to a class of visual learners? Here are some techniques that have worked for me:

• **Exploit the illustrations in textbooks.** The photos and drawings in textbooks are not background decoration that crowd out exercises – they support the written material (if they don't, then choose a different textbook!). Use the art to activate background schema, review vocabulary, and introduce new vocabulary. Ask questions about the pictures (*What do you see in the picture? What is he doing? How is she feeling? What do you think he's going to do next?*). Have students ask and answer questions about the pictures. Have students close their eyes and tell a partner what they remember about the picture.

• **Illustrate new vocabulary words with sketches.** I'm embarrassed to say that I actually asked my husband to give me lessons in drawing stick figures, but it turned out to be an easy skill to acquire, even for the artistically challenged. A quick rudimentary sketch can be far more effective that a verbal explanation. When I can't draw something, I ask for a student volunteer.

• **Use gestures and facial expressions** to explain new vocabulary and demonstrate situations. Illustrations don't have to be drawn on paper. If you're shy about acting something out, use student volunteers ("For extra credit, who can show the class...").

• **Bring in photos, drawings, charts, and graphs** to accompany written materials or lectures. True, this will take some time to prepare, but save your materials in a folder and they'll be ready when you teach the lesson again next term.

• **Encourage students to use graphs and charts to supplement their writing.** Understanding and creating graphs and charts are useful skills for a variety of university classes, and students should learn how to create these with their word-processing and presentation software (and then they can teach you how, if you don't know!).

• **Have students illustrate new vocabulary they're learning.** I have my students create vocabulary cards with the word, context sentence, definition, and original sentence using the word on one side of the card and a picture they've drawn to represent the word on the other side. In the 12 years I've been using this technique, I've never had a student of any age or nationality be unable to illustrate a word or idiom. Students can quiz each other by exchanging sets of cards. Student A shows Student B the picture side of the card and asks A to spell the word, give the definition, and given example sentence; B can check the answer because she is looking at that information while A is looking at the picture.

• **Have students illustrate reading journals**. Ask them to draw quick sketches to illustrate an important scene in a book or some new vocabulary they've learned.

Most importantly, though, teach your classes explicitly about different learning styles. A variety of questionnaires already exist for this, and the good ones also test for kinesthetic learners, social learners, and a variety of other styles. For further reading, check the library for books on this topic by Joy Reid, Kate Kinsella, Mary Ann

Christison, and H. Douglas Brown, among others. It's important for learners not only to understand how they learn best but how to adapt their learning styles to material that is presented in another way.

# I Hate English

I first had Mari, a Japanese student new to the United States, in my fall writing class, and she quickly became one of my favorites. Bright, outgoing, and motivated, she was popular as a partner or group member. She dressed well and took care with her appearance. She turned her assignments in on time, and she did quality work, easily earning an A.

I was pleased, therefore, to see her name on my list the following term for my reading class. This time, however, she didn't shine so brightly. She often seemed tired or listless, and occasionally came to class unprepared. Her absences didn't help her class performance any. I believed her when she said she'd been sick, though, since she often sniffled through class. She no longer dressed up for class, instead wearing the baggy T-shirts and sweatpants that so many other students wear. However, she wasn't a bad student. Her grades hovered around the B level, and she was pleasant enough.

I probably wouldn't have thought about her at all had I not seen such a different version the term before; so I asked her one day during the class break if she felt different from the previous term. I was surprised at how readily she agreed.

"I don't know what's wrong, though," she said. "Maybe it's the rain?" (Well, it *does* rain a lot in Oregon in the winter.)

"Maybe it's culture shock," I suggested.

"Culture shock? What's that?"

What's culture shock? I was amazed that she didn't know. I gave her about a two-minute explanation, but the break was ending, and I didn't have time to go into it in any depth.

Because she'd seemed interested in culture shock, I made a note to bring her something to read. However, while I had taught lessons and units on culture shock in the past, at other institutions, I no longer had any of my old materials. The only thing I had left was a children's book called *I Hate English* (Levine and Bjorkman, 1995). I figured it might be a source of amusement to her, if nothing else.

*I Hate English* tells the story of a Chinese immigrant girl who is unhappy in the United States. The book describes her conflicted and painful emotional reactions to learning a language she doesn't like. I gave Mari the book during break at the next class. She hadn't finished it when class resumed, but she seemed so absorbed that I let her be.

About five minutes later, she burst loudly into tears. Class halted. Mari cried on. I asked her if she wanted to leave the class, but she said no. Well, clearly, this was the time and place for a longer discussion of culture shock. I shelved my lesson plan and outlined the stages:

**Honeymoon:** A newcomer to a foreign country feels almost unnaturally delighted. Everything seems so interesting and wonderful. People in this stage might even declare that they prefer the host country to their native country.

**The crash:** Often occurring nine to twelve months after someone arrives in a foreign country, this stage is the most difficult, and it's the one referred to when someone talks about suffering from culture shock. The person feels unnaturally critical of the host country and all its strange customs. Symptoms can include depression, insomnia, and even a greater susceptibility to colds and minor illnesses.

**Acceptance:** If the person stays in the host country long enough, he or she will probably move on to realize that the new country is neither better nor worse than the native country, just different. While irritants remain, a person in this stage feels more balanced and able to cope.

**Assimilation:** Long-term residents of a foreign country may learn to blend in and negotiate most aspects of daily life with comfort and relative ease.

With Miss Culture Shock sitting right in our midst (still sniffling), it was a perfect time to talk about dealing with the stress. Could, for example, knowing what the stages were prevent culture shock in the first place? I don't think so, though not everyone agreed.

Still, as Mari told us, knowing why she felt so different and unhappy at least reassured her that she wasn't going crazy – and that she wouldn't feel this way forever.

We brainstormed solutions:

• *Seek out friends from your own culture, or, if there aren't any around, other foreigners.* Mari told us that she'd decided when she came to the United States that she would not try to make friends with other Japanese so that she could improve her English more quickly. She looked so relieved to hear that perhaps a Japanese friend was just what she needed – and several Japanese students in the class handed her their phone numbers.

• *Seek out familiar comforts.* Mari hadn't known of the existence of the Asian supermarkets in town where she could buy the foods she missed. We also suggested she read Japanese newspapers online, and call or email friends and family back home.

• *Vent.* Opinions were divided on this. Did openly criticizing things American only drive you deeper into depression, or did it help to let off a little steam? Apparently it depends on the individual. We all agreed, however, that if you did want to criticize, it was best to find a fellow international student to listen (and not, as one student had, unload it all on your host family).

• *Take extra care of your health.* Get enough sleep and eat right.

For me, the lesson from all of this was to remember that students – especially matriculated students who take only a few ESL classes – might not have heard about culture shock. You may have taught something a hundred times, but it could still be a surprise to the next student to walk into your class. No matter what subject area you're teaching, I think it's worth checking in with your class. Culture shock can be discussed, read about, listened to, simulated, and even extended to other areas of life (where it's more often called transition shock), such as marriage, the birth of a child, or getting a new job. You can therefore offer both immediate assistance and teach a life skill at the same time (unless a student really just hates English!).

### Reference
Levine, E., and S. Bjorkman. (1995). *I hate English.* New York: Scholastic.

# Thank You, Mario Pelusi

I hope you'll forgive me if I tell you a story that is not about ESL – at least not directly. I intend to get there in the end, but I'm going to start with something more general, namely the Meaning of Education.

As an undergraduate, I took some courses in music theory and composition. For one class, our final assignment before the semester break was to write a keyboard sonata. It was a somewhat formulaic assignment, but with room for some creativity as well.

I ran into my theory professor in the coffee shop shortly before the assignment was due, and he asked me how it was going.

"Well, I'll finish it in time, but I won't like it," I sighed.

"You won't like it?" He looked distressed, and I assumed he was worried I'd turn in something awful.

"Oh, it'll be correct, don't worry," I reassured him. He still didn't look happy, and he asked what it would take for me to create a composition that I did like.

"About three days of sleep!" I joked.

He then asked if I was going home for the break. When I said that I was, he insisted that I not turn in the composition before I left, but rather that I go home, get my three days of sleep, and then write a composition that I did like and not turn it in until I was happy with it.

I don't know if it was what he said or how he said it, but at that moment, the clouds parted for me, and I truly

Got The Point. He didn't care about my sonata. He'd doubtless heard more than enough student sonatas in his years of teaching. The only person who could possibly care about my sonata was me – and if I wasn't writing it for myself, then I was wasting my time and effort.

That sounds like such a simple concept, and yet at that point, I'd been in school continuously for fifteen years, since age four. I'd attended more than twelve schools in six countries and had studied under scores of teachers and professors, most of them quite good. And yet somehow I'd gotten to be a junior in college without truly understanding that my education was supposed to be meaningful to *me*. Teachers might assign papers and ask questions and distribute grades, but those were just tools they were offering me so that I could progress. Even teachers themselves were tools for me, and I am to this day grateful for that music professor who cared enough about me to get me to care about myself.

When I started teaching, then, I dreamed of leading my own students to similar realizations. But it wasn't that simple. Unfortunately, you can't just tell a class, "Hey! This is the meaning of education!" and have them get it. Not that I didn't try. A student would say, "Thank you, teacher, for giving me an A!" and I'd say, "I didn't *give* it to you – you *earned* it."

"Yes, thank you, teacher" – but no light in the eyes. Once or twice I even tried relating my experience with the sonata, but students always drew the wrong conclusion: "You mean our paper is not really due on Friday?"

So I shifted from trying to explain the overarching purpose of education in general to explaining the aim of much smaller details, such as what we are learning in each chunk of class time and why we are learning it in a certain way.

I keep my explanations short and sweet:

*Why work in pairs?* So students can practice both question forms and answer forms.

*Why study topic sentences?* Because the sample essays showed that most students didn't write strong topic sentences, and I know they'll need this skill in their college classes.

*Why skip chapter 7, the process essay?* Because we don't have time to cover all of the chapters, and I feel the others are more useful.

*Why play a vocabulary game?* Because students seem tired, it's a rainy November day, and I want to practice the material in an enjoyable way.

Some of this no doubt seems very elementary; we've been putting students in pairs for so long that we don't necessarily stop to think about why we do it. But students may genuinely have no idea why they're practicing in this way. Our thousandth English class could still be a student's first.

I like to think that articulating this level of purpose helps my students. I know it helps me. It was exhausting at first to try to justify everything I did. However, I found myself making better choices. After all, if I can't think of a good reason to do something, then I probably shouldn't be doing it. And in time, it became much easier to explain my choices and actions to myself and my students.

From time to time, I also add short explanations to

questions of larger scope: *Why study how to read in English? Why use process writing? Can listening strategies really make a difference?* And I weave into my classes opportunities for students to discuss broader purposes: *What do I want from my education? How will knowing English help get me there?*

I honestly don't know if these techniques get more students to see the light. I do think it makes my classes clearer for students, and it definitely makes classes easier to teach, so I would recommend the practice to anyone. I know, though, that at age nineteen, although I could acknowledge to myself that I finally got the point of education, it didn't occur to me to let my music professor know this, even though I studied with him for another three semesters. He's probably still teaching somewhere, unaware of how much impact he had on my education, my career, and my life – just as your students may not be telling you about the impact you're having on them. Who knows? Perhaps in twenty years, you'll be reading an article like this about yourself.

# Plan B

I called the conference organizer again.

"I'm now in the Las Vegas airport," I said, "and my luggage isn't with me. Do you think you could get me a copy of *Shopaholic Takes Manhattan* and 24 tube socks?"

I could tell Jo Pamment, chair of the Michigan ESL Professional Advisory Committee, was a veteran teacher, because she didn't miss a beat.

"Yes, I can do that for you."

She didn't ask why I needed them, or even why I was in Las Vegas – which would have been a reasonable question because she knew my flight had been booked from Eugene, Oregon, through San Francisco and Chicago to Lansing, Michigan.

But when a mechanical failure grounded my flight out of Eugene, I had to revise my original plans. If I'd waited for the airline to rebook the flight, I wouldn't have made it out of Eugene that day and would therefore have missed the workshop I was supposed to be giving at the other end of the country the following day. So when I saw a line of people boarding a plane, I didn't hesitate. I plunked my credit card down on the counter and asked if I could buy a ticket. As the clerk ran my card, I asked where the flight was going. Well, Las Vegas was at least on the way, and I figured I'd deal with the next connection when I got there.

I finally made it into the Lansing airport a little after midnight. My luggage was about a day behind, so I did the workshop in my comfy (if not terribly attractive) travel dress and running shoes. Fortunately, I had been carrying many of my materials with me. Ms. Pamment had rustled up my requested replacements, and I did without the rest.

As I shared my story with the teachers at the workshop and various teaching friends later on, they recounted their own stories of coping with unexpected challenges:

• Cindi Boardman, a teacher at Laney Community College in Oakland, California, once taught when she had laryngitis. She wrote everything she needed – even her jokes – on the board. Her students actually found it an interesting variation on a normal lesson and, of course, learned quite a bit about nonverbal communication at the same time.

• Cathy Day, a professor at Eastern Michigan State University, was once teaching in Puerto Rico. As she turned to write something on the blackboard, she felt her skirt rip up the back seam – from hem to waist. She turned around and, hugging the walls, backed all the way out of the classroom to the secretary's office. The secretary swiftly stapled the skirt back together, and Cathy returned to class.

• A friend who wishes to remain anonymous arrived at class once to find her room in use by another group that wouldn't leave. She herded her students into the student union building and went looking for unused conference rooms. When she found one, she jimmied it open with her credit card. This special skill so impressed her students that they went into class happily.

• When Lida Baker, a freelance materials writer, realized that she had gone into labor during her morning grammar class, she didn't think, "I'd better dash to the hospital." No, she thought, "After all, the class is almost over. . . ." She gritted her teeth, said nothing, and finished teaching. *Then* she drove herself to the hospital. At least she canceled her afternoon class!

And so on. Probably every teacher reading this article has had something unexpected come up and taught through it anyway. You took the wrong book to class? So you borrow a student's book and teach from that. The power cord's not working and you can't deliver your PowerPoint presentation? So you write the information on the board instead. You're showing a DVD and suddenly the volume stops working? So you have students make up their own dialogue and find that it's better than the original anyway. You prepared extensively for Thursday's class – and have only just now realized that it's actually Wednesday? So you make up a lesson (and a surprisingly good one) on the fly.

Why do we do this? Why leap on a plane to the wrong destination, or mime our way through a lesson with no voice, or ignore labor pains? We're not surgeons or firefighters or ambulance drivers. No one's life depends on our being there. And let's be honest, most of our students probably wouldn't mind a canceled lesson every now and then. But we persevere because we believe our work to be important. We believe in the results we'll achieve in each lesson. We believe in the inherent value of what we're doing, to the extent that we take risks, battle adversity, and pull out our Plan Bs without a second thought.

There is a danger, of course – it's possible to take your job too seriously and forget to have an outside life (something that I believe is necessary for emotional balance) or even to injure yourself through stress or neglect. I still remember my husband calling me from the hospital, where he was taken after his motorcycle accident, to ask me if I could drive him to his yoga class because he couldn't drive himself with his shattered elbow. I blush to say that I did drive him and he did teach the class, but we're older now and can see how stupid that was (at least, I can). However, as long as you don't endanger your physical or mental health, you can rejoice in having chosen a profession that inspires you to face whatever challenges arise.

By the way, if you want to know how I teach writing skills with *Shopaholic Takes Manhattan* and 24 tube socks, I invite you to my next workshop or presentation on writing. I promise you, I'll do everything in my power to be there.

### Reference

Kinsella, S. (2002). *Shopaholic takes Manhattan*. New York: Dell.

# Using Metaphors to Examine Language Learning and Teaching

When I was in college, my music theory professor was fond of telling us, "Music is the universal language." That struck us undergraduates as very funny. When one of us said something unclear, someone would ask, "Why don't you try saying that in Universal Language?" Or if we heard a particularly inept musical performance, we'd sigh and say, "Oh, dear, if you can't speak Universal Language, what is left for you?"

Of course, even then we knew what the professor was trying to do: use something we presumably knew a lot about (language) to help us understand what we were trying to learn (music). The language and music tables have now turned for me, though, and I can use something I've done for many years (studying, practicing, and performing music) to help me understand what I currently teach (learning language – which, when you think about it, is pretty much studying, practicing, and performing).

These realizations I've had about learning music seem equally applicable to learning a foreign language:

**Studying**
- Learning music theory helps me appreciate the depth and beauty of what I play and what I hear.
- It's possible to play music without knowing any

theory, but knowing theory makes playing easier.

## Practicing

• Practicing skills (e.g., scales, arpeggios, chords) gives me fluency that I can draw on later for "real" pieces.

• I have to practice repeatedly to sound good.

• I still make mistakes on the easy pieces I thought I had learned by heart.

• I sound better when I express my feelings in addition to playing the notes.

• If I stop practicing a piece, I lose my fluency.

## Performing

• Somehow, I'm always asked to perform before I feel ready.

• Memorizing a piece makes me less nervous about performing it, but if I over-memorize, I can lose myself in a daze.

• I play better when I'm relaxed.

• The audience doesn't mind (or notice) my mistakes as much as I do.

• Minor mistakes don't matter if the focus is on the piece, not on me.

Philosopher Mark Johnson and linguist George Lakoff have been arguing convincingly since the 1980s that metaphors are not just poetic devices that one studies in high school English classes, but rather are fundamental to human thought. In their 2003 afterword to *Metaphors We Live By* (1980), they point out that "how we think metaphorically matters. It can determine questions of war and peace, economic policy, and legal decisions, as well as the mundane choices of everyday life" (p. 243). Calling the metaphor "unavoidable, ubiquitous, and mostly unconscious," they claim that "we live our lives on the basis of inferences we derive via metaphor" (pp. 272–273). In other words, whether we view learning as growth, a journey, a struggle, or a change determines how we actually learn.

For an extended look at how we teach and learn, then, I recommend an extended metaphor, or analogy. The value of drawing an extended analogy is that it helps you see more clearly. Ironically, it's often easier to see something through the lens of something else. Remember the popularity of the book *All I Really Need to Know I Learned in Kindergarten* (Fulghum, 1988)? It didn't actually teach people anything new. Rather, it examined aspects of life that were already widely accepted by its readers (e.g., violence is bad, death is inevitable, friendship is valuable) and, using the analogy of the rules one learns in kindergarten, presented the concepts in a fresh way so that people could contemplate them anew: "Don't hit people. . . . Goldfish and hamsters and white mice and even the little seed in the Styrofoam cup – they all die. So do we. . . . When you go out in the world, it is best to hold hands and stick together" (pp. 6–7).

We teachers work hard at what we do, and we get tired. We're supposed to plan lessons, create worksheets, develop curricula, grade papers, keep up with the research, chase down absent students, attend meetings, choose textbooks, publish papers, review our peers' classes, present at conferences – oh, and deliver engaging lessons, too. And when we get tired, we tell ourselves to focus, concentrate, and try harder. But perhaps what we really need to do is step back, focus differently, and look at the whole picture.

This is where I think metaphors can help. They allow us to see the forest again when we're bumping into the trees. That perspective can be both enlightening and energizing. Our students work hard, too. They attend classes, carry out language tasks, do homework, write papers, prepare and deliver presentations, study grammar, and read textbooks. We consider a class to be successful when students are engaged every minute. More student talk! Less teacher talk! Task-based learning in the student-centered classroom!

No wonder we have to ask the wandering students to concentrate, focus, and stay on task. However, just like their teachers, maybe what students really need sometimes is to step back and consider what it is that they are actually doing, how they are doing it, and what its value is.

Analogies like the one I've drawn to music can be drawn from nearly any field. Think about what you know well – gardening, snowboarding, raising children, driving a car, making pottery, riding horses, surfing, knitting, being a good friend. Create a simple list of truths from one field that you can apply to your teaching (or your own language learning). Then encourage your students to do the same. Present your realizations to your students, and give them the opportunity to do the same – as a journal assignment, a 15-minute in-class writing to share, a small-group discussion, or an individual presentation to the class. Collect analogies from one class of students to present to the next group.

Whether you conduct your students in a symphony of revelation, join your voice to their chorus of realizations, or add the pedal point of experience to their melodies of discovery, I'm sure you and your students can create beautiful music together.

## References

Fulghum, R. (1988). *All I really need to know I learned in kindergarten*. New York: Villard Books.

Lakoff, G., & Johnson, M. (1980). *Metaphors we live by*. Chicago: University of Chicago Press.

# That's Cheating!

A lion and a cheetah decided to have a race. The cheetah was faster, but the lion ended up winning. How? I solicit guesses from the class. Invariably, a student suggests that the lion must have cheated, which gives me my opening: "Oh, no, because you see – winners never cheat, and cheetahs never win."

We could do a lot with that joke. We could work on pronunciation (*cheater/cheetah*) or discuss what it teaches us about a form of humor (manipulating a few words of a common phrase), but I prefer to use it as the opening of a discussion on cheating. Is it true that winners never cheat? Is it true that cheaters never win?

Students are usually quick to conclude that the saying is false (and here's a good opportunity to slip in a lesson on supporting your opinions with concrete examples) and move on to discuss why people cheat and why (or whether) doing so is bad. If you have low-level students who won't be able to follow the lion/cheetah opener, start by asking them to list different ways one could cheat on a test. This is a good exercise for any level, actually, because once they've shared the methods they know, they'll either be too embarrassed to try them in your class, or you'll at least know what to watch out for!

Most classes eventually consolidate the reasons for cheating into two categories:

1. The cheater feels unequal to the task.
2. The cheater doesn't respect the assignment.

I think the first is more common. Tests and major assignments induce fear. Even students who are well prepared worry about their performance, and for university students there are obvious consequences to not doing well: a lowered grade; then a lowered grade point average; then the loss of opportunity to enter graduate school, land a good job, and live happily ever after. This last point is exaggerated, but the perception is there nevertheless.

The best way to combat this form of cheating is to sufficiently prepare students. Far better that you limit your syllabus and teach a moderate amount solidly than cover too much too quickly. Additionally, teachers sometimes feel pressure to be entertaining and fresh at the expense of reviewing material thoroughly enough. It's OK for students to be a little bored sometimes if that means they've truly mastered your teaching point.

However, you also need to admit that you can't force students to learn. Although you can – and must – provide every opportunity for students to learn and practice, there comes a time when you have to acknowledge their role in taking responsibility for mastering the material. ESL classes are typically smaller than other university classes, and we ESL teachers get to know our students well. It's hard to watch students not live up to their potential or actually fail. So prompt, praise, encourage, goad, (gently) threaten, push . . . but accept that you cannot, in the end, do students' learning for them.

The second form of cheating is trickier to address. Your best defense is transparency: Be crystal clear in your explanations about why you have given a particular assignment and what its value is. Explain why you are teaching a particular point and what you hope to show students by assessing their achievement. Again, though, not all students will accept your explanations.

It's partly age, I think. Come on, show of hands: Did any of you ever cheat in high school or university? I thought so. And was it ever, perhaps, not because you hated learning or didn't understand the assignment, but just, well, because you could?

It's like a challenge to The System, which – because it is set up to be authoritarian and controlling – almost begs some clever students to circumvent it. You can't cause your students to age any faster. But you can help them recognize whether they're tempted by this type of cheating and then discuss the consequences.

Regarding the consequences, we want students to believe that cheaters "only cheat themselves" and that the true punishment to dodging the assignment is missing the knowledge.

Therefore, make that true in your class by placing less emphasis on punishment and demonstrating what learners could do with the skills being offered and what they'd be missing if they didn't acquire these skills.

I'll finish with the incident from my youth that led me to this conclusion. My high school German teacher was a wonderful man who loved languages. He spoke 17 languages fluently, but this made it hard for him to understand students who were only there because they had to take two years of some language to graduate. He was, to put it mildly, overly trusting. His room was never locked, and he would actually leave the classroom during tests.

During my second year, I stole the test booklet off his desk, photocopied it, and returned it. (Sorry, Mr. Cernicek!) It became my job, before each test, to fill out the tests as if they were worksheets and make copies for my friends. I would make different plausible mistakes on each friend's copy – enough so that our papers were different but we all got an A. Then we'd bring the completed tests into class with us and swap them with the blank tests when he wasn't looking.

In the spring, the teacher announced that he had registered us all to take a national high school German proficiency exam. Although my friends did poorly on the exam, I scored in the 90th percentile.

Filling out the tests and choosing the "mistakes" had actually taught me quite a bit of German – not in the same way that my teacher had intended, but at that moment I realized how pleased I was to have learned some German.

This realization changed me, and I can honestly say I never cheated in college, even though I attended one that frequently gave closed-book, unmonitored take-home exams.

I encourage you therefore to spend less time trying to prevent cheating (and much less time beating yourself up if someone manages to cheat) and more time preparing students for their tasks, pointing out the value of what they're learning and helping them understand the broader value of being in school and gaining an education. But I'd still advise you to lock your office and stay in the room while your students take tests.

# Seven Reasons to Attend the TESOL Convention

If you are reading this in December, then the annual TESOL convention is just around the corner. If you submitted a proposal to present, then you already know whether it has been accepted. If it has, I assume that you are going. This column, then, is for those of you who are wondering whether to go – not only to the TESOL convention but to other local and national conferences as well.

Like many others, I struggle with financing my own way, giving up a week's worth of work while I'm away, and missing my family. However, I consider conference attendance one of the most useful things that I do for myself in terms of professional development.

So here are my seven reasons for attending (though not necessarily in order of importance).

1. **You can learn something.** Back home, the learning you do tends to be focused on the job at hand. A conference provides the opportunity to attend sessions on topics of immediate relevance to your work, but it also affords you an excellent opportunity to attend sessions on topics you've never considered before. If you're not sure what corpus linguistics is all about or what's new in genre studies, here's your chance to attend a session or three. If you teach in a high school, why not go to a sym-

posium on Generation 1.5 learners at the community college level? ESL teachers often wind up teaching classes they didn't anticipate, so the session you attend this year out of pure curiosity could turn out to be quite useful in the future.

2. **It may be the only vacation you get.** When I attend a conference, I'm busy from the time I wake up (too early) until the time I drop into bed (too late), but yes, it does still feel like a vacation of sorts. I'm in a new location. I don't have to make my bed or cook my meals. Even if I bring work with me, I'm not really going to do it. To the alert, there's always food and coffee and drinks on offer. Graduate schools, state affiliates, and interest sections are all having parties. It's not quite the same as relaxing in the Bahamas, but it beats grading papers.

3. **It's a good place to look over materials.** Yes, the publishers' area is a zoo, but there's much to be learned there. We're fortunate to work in a profession in which the salespeople, for the most part, have come from a teaching background, so the people who are eager to show you the latest textbooks can also talk about how they would work in an actual classroom. Take enough time to visit the small publishers as well as the large ones. Talk with other teachers you see standing around about what works for them. If you search high and low and cannot find the book you need, tell every publisher about that as well. Who knows? You could influence future publishing plans.

4. **It will look good for you professionally.** That may sound self-serving, but so what? Most teachers could do with a bit more stumping for themselves. At-

tending conferences boosts your reputation with your home institution and makes you more visible to colleagues elsewhere. You're demonstrating your interest in your field, especially if you are participating actively and it is noticed. You can also bring back information for your institution and your colleagues who couldn't attend.

5. **You'll meet people face to face.** Many of us connect online through interest section and forum e-lists. Conferences are our chance to meet in person. Although I value electronic communication enormously, it's not the same as an actual conversation, and meeting the people you've only known online will strengthen your relationships.

6. **It's a great place to network for jobs and career advancement.** The Job Market Place is an obvious venue in which to look for work if you're actively hunting, but the informal networking you do every time you make small talk in an elevator or sit down next to someone new at a lunch table is invaluable. Graduate school classmates and former colleagues congregate at conferences, so you can also renew old friendships. Those connections sometimes pay off even years down the road. (Now that the annual TESOL convention has been shortened by a day, serious networkers may wish to arrive a day early or stay a day late.)

7. **You'll renew your spirit.** OK, I did save the most important point for last. Although a conference week (or weekend) can be physically exhausting, it can be emotionally uplifting as well. You're surrounded by people who love the same things you do but have a different

perspective. They're not bogged down by your particular challenges, and they might have useful insights into your struggles – just as their problems may seem far easier for you to solve than your own. Let their enthusiasm renew yours.

One of my favorite literary treatments of the liberal arts conference scene is David Lodge's (1984) *Small World*. In the prologue, he compares the modern conference to earlier religious pilgrimages and notes that presenting and attending sessions allows people to *journey to new and interesting places, meet new and interesting people, and form new and interesting relationships with them; exchange gossip and confidences (for our well-worn stories are fresh to them, and vice versa); eat, drink, and make merry in their company every evening; and yet, at the end of it all, return home with an enhanced reputation for seriousness of mind.*

So if you're still making up your mind, spend a little time online searching for bargain air or train fares and cheaper alternatives to conference hotels. Email old friends and colleagues to see who's planning to attend. Sort through the announcements and invitations for events, and start filling out your calendar. Write a quick list of things you'd like to learn or do at a conference. And I hope to see you there!

**Reference**

Lodge, D. (1984). *Small world*. New York: Warner Books.

# My Brief Life as a Nonnative Teacher

When I returned to the United States from Japan, it was to teach ESL at a university in Michigan. That was the job for which I was qualified and the one for which I interviewed. However, a few days before the start of the fall semester, I was approached by the chair of the Foreign Languages Department.

"We were wondering if you would agree to teach the Japanese 101 class," he remarked, not really asking, but seemingly assuming my consent.

"Well, um, the thing is, I don't actually know much Japanese," I replied.

"But you were just there."

"True, but I was there teaching English, and living with my English-speaking family."

"Look, I have a fully enrolled class, and the professor scheduled to teach it just quit. Can you do at least this much?" he asked as he showed me the textbook.

I skimmed it and had to admit that, yes, I knew as much as was planned for the first semester of Japanese, and possibly even a little bit more. Furthermore, if I didn't agree to teach the class, it would be canceled, leaving the Foreign Languages Department with Spanish, French, German, Russian, and Latin, but no Asian languages at all. So I said I'd do it.

I had certainly taken foreign language classes taught by nonnative speakers, but they had all been fluent speakers of the target language at the very minimum and had other qualifications such as formal study, previous teaching experience with that language, long overseas residencies, and perhaps marriage to a native speaker.

I, on the other hand, hadn't even studied Japanese formally for more than a semester and had lived only a few years in Japan – largely spent *not* learning the language.

So it took some nerve to walk into the classroom on the first day. However, I reminded myself – and the surprised students – that what I did have was extensive experience teaching a foreign language as well as access to native speakers (whom I was teaching in my ESL classes), the textbook, and two dictionaries.

The class went well. In fact, I offered the second semester in addition and continued to teach Japanese throughout my stay at that university. One year I even added a 201-202 class for a group of highly motivated students, though we were getting dangerously close to the limit of my own language knowledge. A local Japanese-owned factory in the community called and asked if I'd teach Japanese to the line workers and office staff, and I added a few classes there.

There were certainly challenges to being a nonnative teacher. The most frustrating was finding a suitable textbook. Some of the ones I liked best had extensive explanations in the teacher's edition that were way above my ability to read and understand, so I went with a book I didn't like quite as much but that had explanations in English.

Students often asked questions I couldn't immediately answer, but for the most part they seemed content to wait for the answers. I remember one woman who wanted to describe her Halloween costume to her keypal in Japan and came to ask me for vocabulary help. She prefaced her question with, "Actually, Sensei, I'd be really surprised if you knew these words."

"Yes," I said, "so would I! But I do know how to look them up."

"I know," she smiled, "That's so cool."

How gratifying it was to know that finding answers, rather than just having them, could still be "cool."

I found that I relied far more on outside resources than when I taught ESL. For example, I used other Japanese students for modeling pronunciation and checked with various online lists and groups for grammar and vocabulary help.

I was less familiar with Japanese teaching resources. Some games and activities I used for ESL I could use in Japanese, and I frequently raided my son's collection of toys from Japan (e.g., hiragana blocks, refrigerator magnets, puzzles), but I never amassed a collection of Japanese teaching materials to equal my ESL collection.

However, in spite of the difficulties, I discovered some surprising advantages to being a nonnative speaker:

• Students appreciated being able to talk about the target language in their own language. I was lucky to be teaching a mostly monolingual class of native English speakers. Every semester I had a few students from other Asian countries such as South Korea or Singapore, but their English was better than my Japanese, and they never complained about discussing grammar points in English. When I had taught overseas, I'd always taken pride in keeping classes "just in English," yet looking back, I have to admit that part of the reason I did that was because I had to. Had I been fluent in Japanese, I could have offered my Japanese students more efficient help with their English study.

- I had valuable cultural insights to share with my students because I had approached Japan as an outsider.

- I could offer firsthand experience with studying Japanese, and I could share the techniques that had worked for me as a learner.

- I was, in an odd way, a good model. One student told me he had the courage to spend a semester abroad in our town's sister city after seeing how much Japanese I spoke because, as he said, "If you could do it, I knew I could do it, too."

I'm certainly not arguing that it is better not to be fluent in the language that you're teaching. If you're a nonnative teacher, obviously it is better and easier to know as much as you can of the target language. However, I do believe now that, as long as he or she is a skilled teacher, a non-fluent teacher is better than no teacher at all and that a nonnative teacher even has certain advantages over a native-speaking teacher.

After my experiences at that university, I moved to a different state and taught only ESL classes. However, I confess that I felt a certain nostalgia for the time I spent learning Japanese together with my classes.

# Planning Ahead

Whenever I've taught university ESL courses, I've had to provide a syllabus for each one. The syllabi have varied in extent and format, but all the ones I've seen have included at least basic information such as course objectives, scope, textbook, office hours, and contact information. Some go further and offer a rough outline of the course, and some are even more detailed, giving a week-by-week outline of what will be covered in class.

Given a choice, I'd always preferred the looser type of syllabus because I felt it allowed for more flexibility. If your students are struggling with the material in Unit 4, and you wish to spend more time practicing the language or concepts there, it's more difficult if your students are holding a piece of paper promising that you will start Unit 5 the first week of October.

As far as I could tell, my ESL students had no preference for either a loose outline or a tight schedule. (Frankly, it was hard enough to get them to read the syllabus at all.) When I taught my first French 101 classes, I created a syllabus that best suited my needs. I knew I had a point in the textbook that I had to reach because the following semester's class would begin at a determined section and would be taught by me or any number of other French teachers. From that point, I worked backwards to the beginning and then allotted roughly a week per chunk of material.

About a week after I had passed out this syllabus to

my classes and started teaching, a young woman approached me after class.

"I need to know the dates of all your quizzes and tests," she announced. "They're not here on the syllabus."

What could I say? I didn't even know myself when quizzes would be. To stall, I pointed out the date of the final exam (set by the university) and the week during which I'd scheduled the midterm.

"Yes, but what *day* is the midterm?" she demanded.

"Wednesday," I replied with what I hoped was enough confidence to cover the fact that I'd made that up on the spot.

She wrote it down. "And what days are all the quizzes? I need to know so that I make sure I come to class on those days."

Ah, so that was it. I knew she would not be put off by some pedagogical statement such as "I will give quizzes once I determine that the class has mastered a chunk of material." So I went with the answer that had worked before and said, "Wednesdays. Every week," rashly committing myself to therefore writing, administering, and marking 60 quizzes every week.

She walked away satisfied, and I went off to find another French teacher and look at her syllabus. It was a thing of precision – not only were all quizzes and tests clearly marked, but the material that would be covered in class on each of the 64 days of the semester was written down. Even the page numbers were written down.

I asked the teacher what she did if, for example, students were scheduled to cover pages 91–95 on a certain day but didn't get beyond page 93. She couldn't quite grasp my question. If the class was supposed to get to page 95, then the class got to page 95, whether most students were lost or not. After all, if you didn't get to page 95 on Tuesday, how would you start with page 96 on Wednesday? The whole plan would unravel.

I could see my student's point and the point of a detailed syllabus. If a student has five midterms, it's important to know how many of them fall on the same day. If a student is making choices about which days to attend class (which, as much as it irritates me, is their prerogative), it's important to know what's happening in each class.

But when thinking about the syllabus, the broader issue is a more philosophical question: Does a course exist as something independent that marches on its own schedule and into which students must fit? Theoretically, then, a course could move more quickly than most of the students taking it could follow. Or does a teacher adapt the material to be covered to each group of students sitting in front of her, moving more quickly with some groups and more slowly with others? Theoretically, then, students in two different sections of the same course could cover different amounts of material.

I had two French 101 classes, which met daily, and I did everything in my power to keep them on the same schedule, for my own convenience. But as had always been my experience when teaching two sections of the same ESL course, the classes were not really even, and one pulled ahead. I'm sure if I'd given them both a document that explicitly specified which pages and which bits of language would be covered each day, I would have kept those two classes more together. But would that have been the best way of serving the students?

I realized how fortunate I'd been with the flexibility of my ESL courses. Of course, each course had goals and objectives and was intended to cover a certain amount of material. However, I've never taught under an administration that would have (to my knowledge, anyway) disapproved of my supplementing a class with additional material or spending more time in an area of difficulty if the students in front of me merited that treatment.

I don't have an answer to which is more important, the predictability and accountability of a tightly structured syllabus or the flexibility of a more open one. It's hard to even discuss it without saying, "Well, it depends on . . ." However, I do think it's something that each teacher needs to think about and, if feasible, that teachers need to discuss with each other and their administrators. Once you can articulate your own beliefs, you will be better able to reach the compromise that best serves your situation, yourself, and your students.

# The Mystery of the Perfect Method

When I was a child, I enjoyed a certain series of detective novels whose main characters were a group of teens who existed in some fictional world between high school and the work world, who lived at home but had their own cars, money, and total freedom. In each story in the series, the teens would find the buried treasure, locate the missing heiress, or discover the true identity of the mysterious stranger.

At some point in the beginning of almost every story, a warning would be delivered to the young detectives. It might come wrapped around a rock thrown through the living room window, or be tied to the shaft of a South American arrow shot from behind a tree, or slipped into one's coat pocket in a crowded train station. "Stay away from Lone Pines Farm – or else!" "You're in grave danger. Leave immediately!" "The spirit of the mummy's tomb will curse you!" While lesser sidekicks of the main detectives would be worried and ask to quit the case, our heroes would frown over the message (as if this didn't happen every week) and then declare: "Why . . . I think someone's just trying to scare us away!"

Over the years, I've had warnings from proponents of new methods and current teaching trends. They don't come crashing through my window tied to rocks, fortunately, but are announced in graduate school classes and conference presentations, in journal articles and methodology books, or perhaps by colleagues and supervisors.

"Don't use drills! They're boring!" "Every task must be authentic!" "Writing comments on students' papers is a waste of time – they never read them!" "That activity isn't communicative!"

Which warnings are shot at you depends on your age and your teaching context. It seems to me that most of my warnings have involved communicative language teaching, the approach most likely to be stamped GRAS ("generally recognized as safe") by institutions where I have taught.

As a textbook writer and materials designer, I spend a great deal of time now writing exercises I'm told must seem "authentic" and "communicative." That is, every situation should be as close as possible to something in "real life." Dialogues should sound natural. Speaking activities should be designed to get students to say things they would say outside of the classroom. Reading topics should be of current and high interest to students – preferably every student. Students should write on topics that are personally meaningful.

None of these are bad goals, of course. I want to state very clearly here that I am not against communicative activities or authentic communication. However, I think there's something to be said for the artificial as well, at least in the context of a language classroom.

The classroom is not "real life." Even if we put on costumes and role-play our hearts out while doing our communicative activities, it's still a classroom. Why, though, should this be a disadvantage? Why do we not see it as a tremendous advantage? In real life, students can't listen to a conversation over and over again to see where a misunderstanding occurred. They can't (or at least, they probably shouldn't) repeat a word 30 times until they're satisfied with their pronunciation. Precisely because it is *not* real life, the classroom is a unique and valuable place to study language.

I use many communicative activities when I teach, and I don't write any exercise for a textbook or workbook that I would not use myself and do not believe is useful. However, in the classes that I teach, students also do drills. Sometimes I dress these drills up as games, but sometimes I don't. Students memorize dialogues. They even memorize vocabulary lists. I've been known to give dictations and to have students copy out corrected sentences. Why, students even engage in choral repetitions.

I do these things in class because they work. They work for me, and they've worked for my students. That is, they help students learn English, and learn it efficiently. To me, that is the overarching definition of *authentic,* after all. If a student's purpose is to learn English, then anything that helps him or her learn English is an authentic English-learning activity. These activities prepare students for real-life interactions; they don't need to (and sometimes, in fact, they should not) imitate real life. Just as soccer players stretch and practice kicking and blocking, just as musicians learn scales and chords that will later be integrated into larger pieces, students in my classes learn discrete chunks of language that will later be used to communicate freely.

Now, I can't say this approach would work for everyone. You can't solve the *Mystery of the Perfect Method,* because in the case of teaching and learning, there is no one answer. There is no perfect method for everyone, or even for one teacher for every class. Instead of looking for one answer, look at your career as a series of mysteries. Let different teaching philosophies and approaches be your clues and warnings. Discard techniques that don't work, and try out new techniques that you discover.

If you can't find materials to support what you want to do, create your own. Then take your materials and techniques and apply them to *The Secret of the Silent Oral Skills Class*, *The Clue of the Graduate Teaching Assistant*, *The Mystery of the Surly Reading Class*, or *The Puzzle of the Plagiarized Paper* and solve each mystery as it comes to you, week after week, as the star of your own teaching series.

These essays originally appeared in the column "From A to Z" in TESOL's *Essential Teacher* magazine (no longer in print). Some columns that had to be cut to fit the magazine's word count limits appear here in their full original form.

For more information about the TESOL international association, visit their website at http://www.tesol.org.

*Plan B*, March 2008

*Using Metaphors to Examine Language Learning and Teaching*, June 2008

*That's Cheating!*, September 2008

*Seven Reasons to Attend the TESOL Convention*, December 2008

*My Brief Life as a Non-native Teacher*, March 2009

*Planning Ahead*, June 2009

*The Mystery of the Perfect Method*, October 2009

# About the Author

**Dorothy E. Zemach** taught English, French, and Japanese for over 18 years in Asia, Africa, and the US. She holds an MA in TESL from the School for International Training in Vermont, USA. Now she concentrates on writing and editing English language teaching materials and textbooks and conducting teacher training workshops. Her areas of specialty and interest are teaching writing, teaching reading, business English, academic English, testing, and humor. She is a frequent plenary speaker at international conferences, and a regular blogger for Teacher Talk at http://azargrammar.com.

In 2012, Dorothy launched Wayzgoose Press to publish quality works of fiction and non-fiction. Wayzgoose Press is the proud publisher of the *Fifty Ways to Practice* series for students of English as a Second or Foreign Language, and the *Fifty Ways to Teach Them* series for ESL/EFL teachers.